CUSTOM AND CONFLICT IN AFRICA

Custom and Conflict in Africa

By
MAX GLUCKMAN
Professor of Social Anthropology in the Victoria University of Manchester

BASIL BLACKWELL
OXFORD
1963

First printed 1956
Reprinted 1959
Reprinted 1960
Reprinted 1963

Printed in Great Britain for Basil Blackwell & Mott, Ltd.
by A. R. Mowbray & Co. Limited in the City of Oxford
and bound at the Kemp Hall Bindery

TO

AGNES WINIFRED HOERNLÉ

FOR HER

70TH BIRTHDAY

PREFACE

I GAVE these six lectures on the Third Programme of the British Broadcasting Corporation in the spring of 1955. After some deliberation, I have decided to publish them exactly as I delivered them. I was tempted to write an introduction and conclusion, and to insert at several points further illustrations which, by their significant variation, would have strengthened my main argument. But I have decided that once I began to amend a text which was prepared for broadcasting, I should have begun on the writing of a different kind of book. Enough listeners have written to ask me if the lectures were going to be published to justify their appearance as I delivered them. Therefore I have not even tried to define the two key concepts of my argument, 'conflict' and 'cohesion', since I hoped their meaning would emerge as I discussed them. I have only added a reading list of English books.

My first teacher in anthropology, Mrs. A. W. Hoernlé, planted the key idea of my argument in my mind in Johannesburg in 1931, when we were trying to understand the ceremonies which Zulu women performed to their goddess Nomkubulwana (Lecture 5). Since then I have seen it developed, or implicit, in the works of many of my colleagues—those who have worked outside Africa, as well as those who have worked within it, those whom I have quoted, and those on whom I have indirectly drawn. To them all, I acknowledge my deep indebtedness. I have largely used my own research, not because I thought it better than theirs, but because I felt freer to highlight and suppress my own data, to the extent required by broadcasting.

I am grateful to the British Broadcasting Corporation for the invitation to lecture, which induced me to set out explicitly an important theme which has been developed by modern anthropologists, though, of course, it is also known in other disciplines. Mr. Michael Stephens of the B.B.C. did far more than produce my lectures as broadcasts: he helped me work out the main theme, and he suggested the covering title which drove home the point to me myself. I have often discussed the application of the argument to modern society with Professor Ely Devons, to my great profit.

M. G.

CONTENTS

CUSTOM AND CONFLICT IN AFRICA

I

THE PEACE IN THE FEUD

WHENEVER an anthropological study is made of a whole society or of some smaller social group, it emphasizes the great complexity which develops in the relations between human beings. Some of this complexity arises from human nature itself, with its varied organic and personality needs. But the customs of each society exaggerate and complicate this complexity. Differences of age, sex, parentage, residence, and so on, have to be handled somehow. But customary forms for developing relations of kinship, for establishing friendships, for compelling the observance through ritual of right relations with the universe, and so forth—these customary forms first divide and then reunite men. One might expect that a small community, of just over a thousand souls, could reside together on an isolated Pacific island with a fairly simple social organization. In fact, such a community is always elaborately divided and cross-divided by customary allegiances; and the elaboration is aggravated by what is most specifically a production of man in society: his religion and his ritual. In his *Notes towards a Definition of Culture*, Mr. T. S. Eliot saw the importance of these divisions. He wrote: 'I . . . suggest that both class and region, by dividing the inhabitants of a country into two different kinds of groups, lead to a conflict favourable to creativeness and progress. And . . . these are only two of an indefinite number of conflicts and jealousies which should be profitable to society. Indeed, the more the better: so that everyone should be an ally of everyone else in some respects, and an opponent in several others, and no one conflict, envy or fear will predominate. . . .'

'I may put the idea of the importance of conflict within a nation more positively', he goes on, 'by insisting on the importance of various and sometimes conflicting loyalties.' This is the central theme of my lectures—how men quarrel in terms of certain of their customary allegiances, but are restrained from violence through other conflicting allegiances which are also enjoined on them by custom. The result is that conflicts in one set of relationships, over a wider range of society or through a longer period of time, lead to the re-establishment of social cohesion. Conflicts are a part of social life and custom appears to exacerbate these conflicts: but in doing so custom also restrains the conflicts from destroying the wider social order. I shall exhibit this process through the working of the feud, of hostility to authority, of estrangements within the elementary family, of witchcraft accusations and ritual, and even in the colour-bar, as anthropologists have studied these problems in Africa.

All over the world there are societies which have no governmental institutions. That is, they lack officers with established powers to judge on quarrels and to

THE PEACE IN THE FEUD

enforce their decisions, to legislate and take administrative action to meet emergencies, and to lead wars of offence and defence. Yet these societies have such well-established and well-known codes of morals and law, of convention and ritual, that even though they have no written histories, we may reasonably assume that they have persisted for many generations. They clearly do not live in unceasing fear of breaking up in lawlessness. We know that some of them have existed over long periods with some kind of internal law and order, and have successfully defended themselves against attacks by others. Indeed, they include turbulent warriors who raided and even terrorized their neighbours. Therefore when anthropologists came to study these societies, they were immediately confronted with the problem of where social order and cohesion lay.

I myself have not had the good fortune to study in detail such a society, in which private vengeance and self-help are the main overt sanctions against injury by others, and where this exercise of self-help is likely to lead to the waging of feuds. Both my own main fields of research have lain in powerful African kingdoms, where the processes of political control are akin to those patently observable in our own nation. But this lack of personal experience of a feuding society does enable me, without vanity, to bring to your attention what I consider to be one of the most significant contributions which social anthropological research has made to our understanding of social relations. Anthropologists have studied the threatened outbreak of feuds—I say 'threatened outbreak', because nowadays the presence of European governments usually prevents open fighting. But these anthropologists have been able to see the situations which give rise to internecine fights, and, more importantly, to examine the mechanisms which lead to settlements. The critical result of their analysis is to show that these societies are so organized into a series of groups and relationships, that people who are friends on one basis are enemies on another. Herein lies social cohesion, rooted in the conflicts between men's different allegiances. I believe that it would be profitable to apply these analyses to those long-distant periods of European history when the feud was still apparently the main instrument for redress of injury.

But the analysis of feuding societies does not exhaust its interest when we see feud working as a specific institution where there is no government. As I have said, I myself have done research in African kingdoms; and I found it greatly illuminated my analyses of these kingdoms, when I sought in them the processes which my colleagues had disentangled from feuding. Underneath the patent framework of governmental control which organized the state, I found feud and the settlement of feud at work. Permanent states of hostility, like feuds, existed between sections of the nation. These hostilities were redressed by mechanisms similar to those which prevent feuds from breaking out in perpetual open fighting. The same processes go on around us within our own nation-state, and in international relations. I am going in this first lecture to look at how feuding arises and is restrained in African societies which have no governmental institutions. I shall also indicate this evening, what value this analysis has in helping us to understand our own society. In my other five lectures I shall develop the lessons I set out in examining 'the peace' which is contained in the feud.

The working of the threat of private vengeance and the feud has to be exhibited in a detailed analysis of a single society. Our first study of this situation in Africa was made by Professor Evans-Pritchard among the Nuer, a pastoral people of the Upper Nile region. He himself did not organize his analysis primarily to present the argument in which I am interested now, so I am going to describe the Nuer with a slightly different emphasis from his own.

The Nuer dwell in the vast plain which lies around the main rivers in the southern Anglo-Egyptian Sudan. This plain floods in the monsoon rains until it is a great lake, which compels the Nuer to retreat with their cattle on to patches of higher ground where they build their permanent villages and cultivate a hazardous crop of millet. After the rains, the flood falls, and young people spread widely with the herds on the exposed revived pastures, since watering the beasts is easy. But the waters drain away rapidly, and the plain then becomes a dry, scorched waste. The Nuer and their cattle in these most arid months have to congregate again at those low-lying spots where water is retained, either in pools or in the dried-up beds of rivers. Thus groups of Nuer move in rotation between wet-season and dry-season homes. Groups which are separated by miles of flood in one month, some time later may be camping together at a single water-hole; and to reach this they may have had to drive their cattle through the territories of yet other groups. It is therefore essential for these various

groups to be on some sort of friendly terms with one
another, if they are to maintain their cattle, and
themselves, alive. These ecological necessities force
people to co-operate; and this helps to explain how
the Nuer can be organized in tribes of 60,000 people
and more, without any kind of instituted authority.

The Nuer have a very simple technology. Their
country lacks iron and stone, and has few trees to
provide wood for manufactures. They not only
depend on their cattle for much of their food, but also
they make important goods from cattle-skins, horns,
and bones. Since rinderpest reduced their herds, they
live at best just above subsistence. 'It is wistfully
related in one of their stories', writes Evans-Pritchard,
'how once upon a time man's stomach led an independent life in the bush, and lived on small insects roasted
by the firing of the grasses, for (Nuer say) "Man was
not created with a stomach. It was created apart
from him." One day Man was walking in the bush
and came across Stomach there and put it in its present
place that it might feed there. Although when it
lived by itself it was satisfied with tiny morsels of food,
it is now always hungry. No matter how much it eats
it is soon craving for more.' This tale must suffice
to show how near the Nuer live to starvation. Food
supplies are always short. Particular households and
even small areas may suffer severe shortage because
of cattle disease or loss of crops. They have to turn
to others for help. Again, custom requires that when a
man marries he gives forty cattle to his bride's relatives;
thus his own family may become short of cattle. He has
to turn to others for help. The narrow margin of
subsistence, and natural and social vicissitudes which

cause crops to fluctuate in quantity and cattle in numbers, drive Nuer to associate with others if they are to live. But lest you picture a depressed and down-trodden people I must add that the Nuer were fiercely independent warriors, who resisted the advance of the Dervishes and whom the British in the end subdued by bombing their cattle from the air, while the Nuer were themselves steadily invading the territories of other tribes and raiding these for cattle. They are as bellicose among themselves.

The narrow limits of Nuer economy thus force them to associate in fairly populous groups for the production and distribution of food. In these groups they form hamlets and villages, residing in districts whose inhabitants must for most of the time be in some sort of peace with one another. Between some districts there must also be sufficient ties of friendship for their members to cross each other's areas in their moves between flood-season and dry-season homes. The ecological needs for this friendship and peace lessen as the distance grows greater, until, between districts at the extreme ends of a tribe, it hardly exists. Between the different tribes big rivers or wide stretches of un-inhabitable country form natural obstacles and political boundaries. Evans-Pritchard brings out strongly the close relation between the political organization of the Nuer and the lie of their land and the way in which they exploit that land.

There are no chiefs in Nuerland, but in each tribe there is an agnatic clan of aristocrats, a large number of men related to one another by genealogical descent through males from a common founding ancestor. Not all the members of a clan dwell in the tribe where they are aristocrats, and each tribe contains members of many clans. The various districts of a tribe are held to be linked together by their place on the clan genealogy. It works this way. Two neighbouring districts are associated through two long-dead brothers, while another three neighbouring districts are associated through another set of three brothers, whose father was brother to the father of the first set. In this way, the various districts of a Nuer tribe link up in larger and larger sections by being grouped with more distant ancestors of the tribe's aristocratic clan. If one district is involved in fighting, those related to it in brotherhood unite with it against its enemies, who will be joined by their brother-districts. But if one of them is involved in fighting with a more distant section all these districts may join up with one another. While they are thus allied, feuds among themselves fall under truce. These large districts are therefore composed of sections which may at times be hostile to one another, but unite against a more distant enemy. Ultimately all Nuer tribes are united against foreigners; when foreigners are not involved, they split into feuding primary sections, which may, when not fighting each other, split into smaller hostile sections, and so on. The process is not dissimilar from the groupings of nations which in European history have allied against enemies, and then split apart after victory.

In this process of what Evans-Pritchard calls *fusion* of sections against larger groups, and *fission* into sections when not involved against those larger groups, the Nuer recognize certain changes in the rules of war. Men of the same village fight each other with clubs, not spears. Men of different villages fight each other with the spear. There is no raiding within the tribe for cattle, and it is recognized that a man ought to pay cattle as compensation for killing a fellow-tribesman, though this is rarely done. Nuer tribes raid one another for cattle, but not for women and children who must not be killed; nor must granaries be destroyed. When raiding foreign people, women and children and even men can be captured, women and children can be killed, and granaries can be destroyed.

This is all I am going to say about the large-scale political system of the Nuer. Here fighting can go on, and injuries need not be recompensed, because the groups live far apart. The feud can be waged. Peace is not necessary to preserve life. But in more limited areas, because of the crossing of cattle-drives and so forth, men have to be friends if they are to survive. Yet we know only too well, from our own experience, that the necessity of friendship of itself is not enough to achieve friendship. Men quarrel over many things— cattle, land, women, prestige, indeed over accidents. (I've seen two Zulu lock in armed combat because one bumped into another in the excitement of a war-dance.) Or if men don't quarrel, they have differences of opinion about the rights and wrongs of a contract, and these differences have to be settled by some rule other than that of brute force, if social relations are to endure. Often, difficulties in dispute arise not over what is the appropriate legal or moral rule, but over how the rule applies in particular circumstances. This is true even of most disputes in our highly developed legal system. In effect, both parties may claim to be in the right, and agreement has to be reached on which is in the right and how far he is in the right. Nuer have an established code of law which sets out, for example, what a man should pay in cattle to get a bride from her father, and what he should pay to his cuckold, or to the kin of a man whom he has slain, or for other offences. They have rules controlling the division of inheritances and of cattle received from the husbands of their kinswomen. That is, they have a code of law, as a series of conventional rules about what is right action, and what is wrongful action. But they haven't any legal procedures or officials, in the sense that there are no authorities charged with summoning disputants, listening to their cases, and enforcing the rules of law against wrongdoers. And as most men tend to feel that they are in the right when the dispute is obscure, and plenty of men are ready to evade their proper obligations if they can, we may well ask how friendship is maintained despite quarrels. It is here that customary ties are important, and the enforcement of those ties by beliefs in ritual punishment. Certain customary ties link a number of men together into a group. But other ties divide them by linking some of them with different people who may be enemies to the first group. For the Nuer, like all peoples, do not exploit their land in haphazard lots of associates, but in organized groups which are broken by relationships which cross-link their members in other relationships.

The most important tie among the Nuer is that of agnatic kinship—kinship by blood through males. I have described how the larger districts are associated together by the idea of this bond of brotherhood and fatherhood. In much smaller groups, the men descended through males from a nearby ancestor form a closely knit corporate unit. They own and herd their cattle together. They inherit from one another. And, above all, if one of their members is killed they must exact vengeance for him against the killer or one of the killer's vengeance group, or they must obtain blood-cattle in compensation for the death from this vengeance group. This is the theory. But in practice, it seems that among the Nuer this group of agnatic avengers does not always reside together—it is not a local community. In fact, the vengeance group may well be widely scattered. Nuer move about frequently for many reasons. They may quarrel with their fellows at home, and so go elsewhere, perhaps to a maternal uncle. Or they may just go to rich maternal uncles. A man's mother may go in widowhood to be a concubine to some man in a distant village, and there her sons grow up, though all of them belong to the dead husband, even if he did not beget them. And the like. This scattering of some vengeance groups means that a conflict arises between the loyalty of close agnates, the tie which above all demands solidarity, and the ties which link a man with his local community, which he must also support by custom as well as from interest. For though vengeance should be taken by the agnatic group, the fellow-residents of this group mobilize in a battle behind it. Now if the vengeance group is scattered it may mean, especially in the smaller districts, that the demand for community solidarity requires that a man mobilize with the enemies of his agnates. And in the opposite situation such an emigrant member of the group which has killed may be living among the avengers, and be liable to have vengeance executed upon him. I suggest (because Evans-Pritchard does not mention this point) that his exposure to killing exerts some pressure on his kin to try to compromise the affair. In addition, whether he remain where he is or escape home, he is likely to urge his kin to offer compensation, since he has many interests in the place where he resides. Conversely, if a man of the group demanding vengeance resides among the killers, he has an interest in securing that his kin accept compensation instead of insisting on blood for blood. Dispersal of the vengeance group may lead to a conflict between local and agnatic loyalties, and divide each group against itself.

Divisions of purpose in the vengeance group are created above all by marriage rules. Practically every society in the world insists that there should be no mating within the family of parents and children. I think the only exceptions are certain royal families. Many societies extend the bans on marriage outside the family itself, to more distant kin. This is the rule anthropologists call 'exogamy'—marriage-out. Among the Nuer, the rules forbid, under penalty of disease, accident, and death, a man to marry any woman of his clan, or any woman to whom relationship can be traced in any line up to six generations. The first rule, banning marriage in the clan, compels the men of each agnatic vengeance group to seek in other agnatic groups for their own wives, and for husbands for their sisters. The rules banning marriage to other sorts of kin compel the members of each group to spread their marriages widely through, one assumes, practically every agnatic group in the local community. To marry thus requires first of all some kind of friendship with those other groups. Some African peoples say of groups other than the one to which they belong, 'They are our enemies; we marry them'; but after marriage there is a sort of friendship, though it differs from the main blood-tie. More than this, when a man has got a wife from another group, he has an interest in being friends with that group which his fellow-agnates do not have, though they too regard his in-laws as relatives. Their wives make them friendly with other groups. It's not just sentiment. A woman remains attached to her own kin, and if her husband quarrels with them she can make life pretty unpleasant for him. But her ancestors are also able to affect her and her children, and hence her husband's well-being. A man's brother-in-law is maternal uncle to his children, and by custom is required to assist them in many critical situations. He can bless his nephew, and his curse 'is believed to be among the worst, if not the worst, a Nuer can receive, for, unlike the father, a maternal uncle may curse a youth's cattle, as well as his crops and fishing and hunting, if he is disobedient or refuses a request or in some other way offends him. The curse may also prevent the nephew from begetting male children.' So for the welfare of his family, and the prosperity of his children, each man is led by his interests, and compelled by custom, to seek to be on good terms with his wife's kin. And he has, as the child of a woman from yet another group, an interest in being on good terms with his own mother's kin. Again, this interest is supported by customary rights to get help, and by the danger of suffering mystical retribution if he does not conform with these customs. The fact that men of a single group of agnates have mothers from different other groups, and marry wives from still other groups, strikes into the unity of each vengeance-group. The loyalty of agnates to one another, so strongly enforced by custom, conflicts with other customary allegiances to other groups and persons. Some members of each warring group have an interest in bringing about a settlement of quarrels. And these differences of loyalty, leading to divisions in one set of relationships, are institutionalized in customary modes of behaviour, and are often validated by mystical beliefs. Thus where custom divides in one set of relationships, it produces cohesion, through settlement of quarrels, in a wider range of social life.

Underlying these customary divisions, which put pressure on the parties to settle a dispute, is the constant pressure of common residence. For common residence implies a necessity to co-operate in maintaining peace, and that peace involves some recognition of the demands of law and morality. It also involves mutual tolerance. These demands are backed by the constant intermarriages which go on in a limited area, since men do not commonly seek wives from afar. Hence the Nuer as individuals are linked in a wide-flung web of kinship ties which spreads across the land; and new meshes in this web are constantly being woven with each fruitful marriage. These webs of ties, centring on individuals, unite members of different agnatic groups. And always local groups have common local interests.

These common local interests are represented by a category of arbitrators, who may be called on to help settle disputes. The arbitrators are ritual experts who are called 'men of the earth'. They have no forceful powers of coercion. They cannot command men to do anything and expect them to obey; but they are political as well as ritual functionaries. If a fight breaks out, the 'man of the earth' can restore peace by running between the combatants and hoeing up the earth. The slayer of a man is defiled with blood, and can neither eat nor drink until the 'man of the earth' has let the blood of the dead man out of his body. If the slayer resides near the home of the man he has killed, he will live in sanctuary with the 'man of the earth' to avoid death at the hands of his victim's kin. The 'man of the earth' will then negotiate between the two groups, and try to induce the deceased's kin to accept compensation. This they are bound in honour to refuse; but eventually they will yield when the 'man of the earth' threatens to curse them. Evans-Pritchard himself never observed this process; but he collected tales of the dire effects of such a curse.

He found that 'within a village differences between persons are discussed by the elders of the village and agreement is generally and easily reached and compensation paid, or promised, for all are related by kinship and common interests. Disputes between members of nearby villages, between which there are many social contacts and ties can also be settled by agreement, but less easily and with more likelihood of resort to force.' Between sections on extreme sides of a tribe, chances of settlement are less. Hence, Evans-Pritchard says, 'law operates very weakly outside a very limited radius and nowhere very effectively'. But he shows that there is a law, and as we see it is represented in the person of the 'man of the earth'. This functionary also represents the need for communal peace over a certain area. Customary practices here again divide men, by emphasizing the disturbance after a homicide: the kinsmen of killer and victim cannot eat or drink together, and they may not both use the dishes of third parties. It sounds as if some husbands and wives might not be able to eat together. In fact, to conceal that one has killed a man is a dreadful offence because it is believed to put the whole district under threat of mystical disaster. Clearly people cannot go to their gardens or pastures in any security. Some adjustment must be made. It is here that the 'man of the earth' acts, through his connection with the earth. It seems that for the Nuer, as for many African societies, the earth has a mystical as well as a secular value. The secular value of the earth lies in the way it provides for the private interests of individuals and groups within the larger society. They make their living off particular gardens, pastures, and fishing-pools; they build their homes, make their fires, and eat their meals on their own plots of ground; they beget and rear their children on the earth. Their ancestors are buried in the earth. Men and groups dispute over particular pieces of earth to serve these varied ends. But men live, work, dance, breed, die, on the earth in the company of other men. They obtain their rights to earth by virtue of membership of groups, and they can only maintain themselves by virtue of this membership. To live on the earth they require friendship with other men over a certain area. The earth, undivided, as the basis of society, thus comes to symbolize not individual prosperity, fertility, and good fortune; but the general prosperity, fertility, and good fortune on which individual life depends. Rain does not fall on one plot, but on an area; locust swarms and blights and famine and epidemics bring communal disaster, and not individual disaster alone. With this general prosperity are associated peace and the recognition of a moral order over a range of land. In West Africa men worship the Earth, and in this worship groups who are otherwise in hostile relations annually unite in celebration. In Central and South Africa kings, who symbolize the political unity of tribes, are identified with the earth: the Barotse word for king means 'earth'. And in some African tribes there is a dogma that the king must be killed when his physical powers decline, lest the powers of the earth decline simultaneously. Among the Nuer, the ritual expert who is connected with the earth, in its general fertility, and who therefore symbolizes the communal need for peace and the recognition of moral rights in the community of men, acts as mediator between warring sections.

What emerges, I think, is that if there are sufficient conflicts of loyalties at work, settlement will be achieved and law and social order maintained. It is custom which establishes this conflict in loyalties. Men are tightly bound by custom, backed by ritual ideas, to their agnatic kin. Ritual ideas sanction the customary ties to maternal kin. As we follow Evans-Pritchard's analysis, working outwards from the individual Nuer into the larger Nuer society, we see that at every point each man is pulled into relations with different men as allies or enemies according to the context of situation. A man needs help in herding his cattle: therefore he must be friends with neighbours with whom he may well quarrel over other matters—or indeed over the herding of cattle. The herding of cattle demands that certain separated groups at some seasons be in amicable relations. A man cannot, under stringent taboos, marry his close female relatives: this means that he must be friendly enough with other people for them to give him a wife. He marries her in elaborate ceremonies and transfers cattle which he collects from all his kin and gives to all her kin. These elaborate ceremonies and payments of cattle establish friendships for him. And through his wife he strikes up alliances with relatives-in-law which are inimical to a whole-hearted one-sided attachment to his own brothers and fellow-members of his clan. His children have close ties of sentiment with the kin of their mother. Custom supports these ties with obligations and mystical threats. A man's blood-kin are not always his neighbours: the ties of kinship and locality conflict. And all these ties, I repeat, are elaborately set in custom and backed with ritual beliefs.

These allegiances, and a man's allegiance to his community and its sense of right-doing, create conflicts which inhibit the spread of dispute and fighting. There is a conflict between a man's desire to serve his own material ends, ruthlessly, and his recognition of a code of law and right-doing under that code; and this conflict appears in his kinsmen's willingness or un-willingness to support him in a quarrel. There is a conflict between the assertiveness of each individual and kin-group and the interests which induce them to come to terms with their neighbours. This is the conflict which is resolved through the ritual curse of the 'man of the earth'. Custom lays down the code of law which establishes the nature of right-doing, and custom ordains that men shall recognize ties of varying kinds of kinship, or of locality, or of several other sorts. But custom is effective in binding the Nuer into a community which maintains some kind of order—what Evans-Pritchard calls 'ordered anarchy'—because the obligations of custom link men in different kinds of relationships. Over longer periods of time and wider ranges of society the conflicts between these relationships become cohesion.

I may have given the impression that I am arguing that vengeance is never taken and the feud is never waged. I don't want to do this. Feud is waged and vengeance taken when the parties live sufficiently far apart, or are too weakly related by diverse ties. Even when they are close together, hot-headedness and desire for prestige may lead to vengeance and constant fighting. But where they are close together, many institutions and ties operate to exert pressure on the quarrellers to reach a settlement. Again, this is not to say that settlement of quarrels is always achieved. We must remember that quarrels arise out of the very ties which link men—ties with one's wife's kin or one's own kin or one's neighbours. There is only pressure towards the establishing of peaceful relations—or, rather, the re-establishing of peaceful relations after a breach. This pressure is exerted by common interest in a modicum of peace over a certain area, which is necessary if men are to live in any kind of security, and produce food, marry into one another's families, or deal with one another. The conflicts between the loyalties held by a man thus, in a wider range of relations, establish order and lead to recognition and acceptance of obligations within law. A man's several loyalties strike at the strength of his loyalty to any one group or set of relationships, which is thus divided. Hence the whole system depends for its cohesion on the existence of conflicts in smaller sub-systems. Each vengeance group of agnatic kinsmen is divided by the different maternal and conjugal and local attachments of individual members.

Clearly the primary source of division in the groups of kin which are characteristic of primitive society, is the rule that men must not marry their clanswomen and other near relatives. But many societies by custom prefer marriage with certain sets of kin, and therefore these show a different working of the political process. In one society, that of the Bedouin of Cyrenaica, marriage is allowed within the vengeance group itself by Islamic law. The analysis of the resulting situation, and its connection with habitat, will be a good test of the above argument. Dr. Emrys Peters is at present occupied with this study. We know that there are societies where feuds occur in comparatively small areas; but none of these have been subjected to adequate anthropological analysis in terms of the many ties established by custom.

Later studies have supported the main points made by Evans-Pritchard about Nuer society. I make brief reference only to one study. Evans-Pritchard himself emphasized the positive aspects of ties linking members of agnatic vengeance groups to other groups: I have myself argued that they have a divisive effect within the group, and this is where the emphasis was placed by Dr. Elizabeth Colson in her study of the Tonga of Northern Rhodesia. I can't present the beauty of her study, but I give a summary statement of a case she recorded—this is the clearest case of the working of the vengeance threat which we have from Africa. A man of the Eland clan killed a man of the Lion clan. The murderer was arrested by the British and sent to gaol: but the Lions broke off all relations with the Elands who lived nearby. Eland men in Lion villages, and Lion men in Eland villages, told Miss Colson that in the past they would have fled home: as it was, the Lions ostracized their Eland fellow-villagers. Eland women living with Lion husbands among the husbands' kin were subject to insults and threats— which upset the husbands. The Elands proffered compensation through joint in-laws of themselves and the Lions; peace was made, and blood-cattle promised to compensate for the homicide. The Elands were slow in paying. Eventually, a son of an Eland woman by a Lion man fell ill and died: the diviner said that the murdered man's spirit had killed the child because cattle had not been paid. The women again began to exercise pressure on male kin to settle the matter. The dispersal of the vengeance group, and the marriages of its women with men of other vengeance groups, produced divisions in the ranks of each group, and exerted pressure for settlement. The death of a child, which custom blamed on the vengeful spirit, created the situation compelling a meeting, at which other relatives of the two parties acted as intermediaries.

The general principle I've been stating has been long recognized by many scholars, but others have over-looked its significance. In their great *History of English Law* Pollock and Maitland wrote that in Anglo-Saxon times 'personal injury was in the first place a cause of feud, or private war, between the kindreds of the wrongdoer and of the person wronged'. The

Shorter Cambridge Mediaeval History says that feud
'produced a state of incessant private warfare in the
community, and divided the kindreds themselves
when the injury was committed by one member
against another of the same group'. I doubt this.
The Anglo-Saxon vengeance group, called the *sib*,
which was entitled to claim blood-money for a dead
man, was composed of all his kindred, through males
and females, up to sixth cousins. But the group which
resided and worked together seems to have been some
form of patriarchal joint family: again we find that the
vengeance group did not coincide with the local
group. And if you trace each man's kin up to his sixth
cousins, they form a widely scattered grouping which
could not mobilize. Each man, with only his full-
brothers and full-sisters, was the centre of his own sib;
and every individual was a member of the sibs of
many other people. Indeed, I venture to suggest that
in a long-settled district, where there had been much
intermarrying, almost everyone would have been a
member of everyone else's sib. Hence where vengeance
had to be taken, or redress enforced, some people would
have been members of both plaintiff and defendant
sibs. They would surely have exerted pressure for
just settlement. This is the position among the
Kalingas of the Philippine Islands who have a similar
kinship system. Feuds may have been prosecuted
between sibs in separated districts, or as battles between
local communities mobilized behind noble families.
But we must not take sagas and tales of feuding as
evidence, for they may, like the tales of the Nuer
'man of the earth's' curse, stand as warnings. Or
even as historical records they may have been better

warnings. There was only one lot of Hatfields and McCoys in the Kentucky and Virginia hills. Generally, over a limited area, there is peace as well as war in the threat of the feud.

This peace arises from the existence of many kinds of relationships, and the values attached to them all by custom. These ties divide men at one point; but this division in a wider group and over a longer period of time leads to the establishment of social order. In separated districts men can quarrel. The smaller the area involved, the more numerous the social ties. But as the area narrows the occasions which breed quarrels between men multiply; and here it is that their conflicting ties both draw them apart, and bring them into relationship with other people who see that settlement is achieved. In this way custom unites where it divides, co-operation and conflict balancing each other. At the widest range, cohesion is stated in ritual terms—supported by mystical retribution— where values are unquestioned and axiomatic. Hence ritual reconciliation and sacrifice often follow the settlement of a quarrel, and ritual methods are used to reach adjustment.

The social process of the feud and threat of feud may seem very distant from us, but in fact it is present on our doorsteps. The application of this analysis to international affairs would overlook many complicating factors: is there a single moral order, for example, as among the Nuer? Can nations allow their members to recognize external conflicting ties of loyalty? There is clearly, as in Nuerland, an increasing technological necessity for some kind of peace over all the world. That I leave aside. I would, however, argue that it is

C

useful to look at our own national life in these terms. If we examine the smaller groups which make up our vast and complex society, it is easy to see that divisions of interest and loyalties within any one group prevent it from standing in absolute opposition to other groups and to the society at large. For men can only belong to a large society through intermediate smaller groups, based on technical process, on personal association, on locality, on sectarian belief within a larger cult, and so forth. Schools which are organized in houses cutting across forms, and Universities which have colleges cutting across departments and faculties, exhibit more cohesion than amorphous schools and universities. Tight loyalties to smaller groups can be effective in strengthening a larger community if there are offsetting loyalties.

The feud is, according to the dictionary, 'a lasting state of hostility'. There is no society which does not contain such states of hostility between its component sections; but provided they are redressed by other loyalties they may contribute to the peace of the whole. One group of workers, bound together in a particular process and not immediately involved in a dispute with a factory's employers, may oppose another group's going on strike. Indeed, there is a conflict in the loyalties which operate on each worker and each working-group because of familial and national ties, so that man and group are inhibited from moving into violent action. Every worker has an interest in keeping the factory working at all costs, in addition to an interest in getting as high wages as he can. Or if work stops, he wants it to begin again. Similar divisions exist between employing-groups, and within the ranks of management inside a factory. Nowadays the significant groups in British political life are largely functional groups—trade unions, employers' and trade associations, educational interests, religious sects, and the like. It is these which exert pressure on Parliament, but it is not interest-groups which elect members to Parliament. We therefore get a high degree of national representation because most members of Parliament are elected by amorphous constituencies which contain many of these interest-groups. The Member of Parliament is supposed to represent all his constituents, whatever their party affiliation; and this system of representation cuts clean across the important political pressure groups. He is like the Nuer 'man of the earth'.

Again, I am not suggesting that divided loyalties and interests will always prevent a dispute arising, or prevent social dislocation and change. Loyalties and interests are not thus beautifully balanced. What I am saying is that these conflicting loyalties and divisions of allegiance tend to inhibit the development of open quarrelling, and that the greater the division in one area of society, the greater is likely to be the cohesion in a wider range of relationships—provided that there is a general need for peace, and recognition of a moral order in which this peace can flourish.

I have hinted at where the process of the feud, with its war and its peace, can be detected in Britain. Many people have so detected it; but as many are reluctant to accept the reality of social life—that quarrels and conflicts exist in all groups and cannot be wished out of existence. They must be redressed by other interests and other customary loyalties, so that the individual is led into association with different fellows. The more his ties require that his opponents in one set of relations are his allies in another, the greater is likely to be the peace of the feud.

II

THE FRAILTY IN AUTHORITY

WHEN Macbeth was tyrannizing over Scotland, Macduff in desperation fled to England to beseech Malcolm, the son of murdered King Duncan, to lead an army of liberation against the tyrant. Malcolm feared lest Macduff might be enticing him into the tyrant's hands, so to test Macduff he described himself as a most arrant villain, saying he had no saving graces. He compared his character with that of the ideal king, thus:

>   the king-becoming graces,
> As justice, verity, temperance, stableness,
> Bounty, perséverance, mercy, lowliness,
> Devotion, patience, courage, fortitude,
> I have no relish of them.

There's a list of virtues few human beings can attain. True, they are the virtues of a monarch. But in lesser degree such virtues are required of all leaders. Thus, in another sphere, professors should be learned and scholarly, original research-workers, inspiring teachers, tolerant with students, good administrators.

It follows, therefore, as positions of leadership carry high ideals, and as most men are, well, only men, there develops frequently a conflict between the ideals of leadership and the weakness of the leader. This is the frailty in authority. For it is likely that as a leader exhibits his weaknesses—natural human weaknesses though they be—his subordinates may begin to question his authority, to turn against him, and ultimately to seek someone else who, they fondly imagine, will attain the ideals they desire.

But in certain types of society, when subordinates turn against a leader thus, they may only turn against him personally, without necessarily revolting against the authority of the office he occupies. They aim to turn him out of that office and to install another in it. This is rebellion, not revolution. A revolution aims to alter the nature of political offices and of the social structure in which they function, and not merely to change the incumbents in persisting offices. Aristotle saw this distinction between rebellions and revolutions, and pointed out that rebellions do not attack political authority itself. But anthropologists have developed considerably what is implied in this process. I am going to argue in this lecture that these rebellions, so far from destroying the established social order, work so that they even support this order. They resolve the conflicts which the frailty of authority creates. They also resolve certain other conflicts which arise in other parts of the political system. For rebellious tendencies against authority are restrained by the structure of the political system itself. They are controlled by custom which gives men allegiances to various leaders, so that when they attack one leader, they do it by supporting another leader of the same kind, in the name of the ideals of leadership. That is, as with the feud, the divisions between leaders seeking for power, and between followers seeking for leaders, in terms of interests and customary allegiances which exist in one range of social relations, lead to conflict and even open strife; but over a wider span of space and time these divisions may result in social cohesion.

The simple situation of conflict between the ideals of leadership and human frailty is a profitable starting-point from which to examine the pitfalls which beset authority, and the devices instituted by custom to evade those pitfalls. For if authority be inherently frail, we may well expect its frailty to be accentuated in the complex situations which in real life beset all leaders who, however sagacious they be, cannot always measure exactly all the factors involved. Even less can they control these. Now indigenous African states provide us with fields where we can observe authority acting in comparatively simple situations, and here we have probably the simplest setting for conflict against authority.

In these African states there was no fundamental cleavage of economic interest between rulers and subjects. Individual acts of tyranny may have been numerous, but there was rarely any systematic exploitation by the tyrant of the labour of his subjects. We all know how strongly Dr. Livingstone preached and fought against the export slave-trade in Africa. Yet this is what he said of the domestic slavery within African tribes in the interior: 'Among the coast tribes [in touch with slavers] a fugitive is always sold, but here [in the interior] a man retains the same rank he held in his own tribe. The children of captives even have the same privilege as the children of their captors.' 'The Rev. T. M. Thomas,' Livingstone goes on, 'a missionary now living with [chief] Moselekatse, finds the same system prevailing among his Zulus or Matabele. Mr. Thomas says that "the African slave, brought by a foray to the tribe, enjoys, from the beginning, the privileges and name of a child, and looks upon his master and mistress in every respect as his new parents. He is not only nearly his master's equal, but he may, with impunity, leave his master and go wherever he likes within the boundary of the kingdom: although a bondman or servant, his position, especially in Moselekatse's country, does not convey the true idea of a state of slavery; for, by care and diligence, he may soon become a master himself, and even more rich and powerful than he who led him captive." ' Livingstone went on to say: 'The practice observed by these people, on returning from a foray, of selling the captives to each other for corn or cattle, might lead one to imagine that slavery existed in all its intensity among the native Africans; but Mr. Thomas, observing, as I have often done, the actual working of the system, says very truly, "Neither the punctuality, quickness, thoroughness, nor amount of exertion is required by the African as by the European master" '.

Many other writers who were in South and Central Africa at this period have underlined the limitations of the economic system and their effect on political relations. Shaka, the head of the small Zulu tribe, by conquest built up a great kingdom in the Natal region. But as he raided tribe after tribe and amassed vast herds of cattle, he could not use these to raise his own standard of living: he ate the same boiled beef as his followers, and having many cattle he gave most to his subjects for them to eat as boiled beef. He too, like his subjects, lived in a pole-and-grass hut. Limited trade relations inhibited the introduction of luxuries; and relatively inefficient tools prevented those who had control of labourers from putting them to great productive use. When the Zulu king Shaka built a new capital he sent thousands of warriors to fetch a sapling each from unnecessarily distant forests. Not even the first introduction of firearms and European trade-goods broke up this egalitarianism. A band of Nyamwezi freebooters with muskets established an empire over the Katanga tribes, under a tyrant named Msidi. This is what a missionary wrote, after Msidi was killed: The people 'don't study that aspect of Msidi's life which pictures him as thundering out the death warrant . . . and even tasting from his executioner's hand the warm life-blood of his dying victim; but they recall how he would show himself to be kindness and liberality itself, and how he would wear, day in and day out, a miserable two yards of dirty calico and yet would give away, to the last yard, the bales upon bales of cloth brought into the country by the many caravans from east and west coasts'.

Rich there were, and the poor suffered greater shortages of food; but the main interest of the rich lay in building up bands of followers by giving them land for which they had no other use, and feeding them from surplus stocks of cattle and grain. There are no complicating conflicts arising from clashes of economic interest between classes. There are such clashes between individuals and groups, however, and I want to examine how they arise out of customary arrangements and are handled by other customary arrangements. I am trying here to emphasize that in these African kingdoms we are able to analyse conflicts as they are created by the system of authority itself.

I take a fairly simple state, that of the Zulu, which I have myself studied.

Zululand is now the north-eastern part of the South African Province of Natal. Like the rest of Natal, it is a pleasant country of rolling hills, watered by rivers flowing down from the highland massif of the Drakensberg. They run through narrow valleys which broaden towards the sandy coastal plain along the Indian Ocean. The tales of mariners shipwrecked on this coast give us some idea of the political system which prevailed in the region during the sixteenth to eighteenth centuries. It is a picture of a fairly populous system of small independent tribes, under chiefs. The tribes were mostly at peace with their neighbours, though they fought short wars and raided one another for cattle. But no chief attempted to extend his rule over his neighbours, and tribes were constantly splitting and migrating.

This picture began to change during the last quarter of the eighteenth century. The change may have been brought about by wars farther to the south-west, where the Boer colonists in their expansion had begun to drive back the frontier tribes. This fierce impact may have run back through all the tribes.

At any rate, from this period tribes began to fight with one another for dominance, and the stronger groups extended their rule over their neighbours. These dominating groups then fought each other, until in 1818 the Zulu emerged as the supreme power in the region. They devastated large areas of land, and some of their defeated enemies started on careers of conquest which disturbed Africa as far as Lake Victoria Nyanza, thousands of miles away. These migrant groups were still involved in fighting at the end of the nineteenth century, when European colonization ended this phase of Africa's warfare.

In their first conquests the Zulu were led by Shaka, and from his reign onwards we have fair accounts of Zulu life. English traders and missionaries settled in Natal, and Boer trekkers entered it a few years later. Shaka was himself assassinated by two of his brothers ten years after he established his final supremacy in the region. One of these brothers killed the other, and was in turn defeated by another brother. It is a familiar story of brothers fighting for the throne. The kingdom then settled into comparative internal peace, but internecine fights continued. In 1880 the British conquered Zululand. I am going to look at rebellion in this short-lived kingdom.

Like many other African states, and states in other lands, the Zulu kingdom was divided into counties. These counties were regions with defined boundaries. Some of them were composed of formerly independent tribes which had been brought under the authority of the Zulu king; others were made up of fragments of these independent tribes collected and placed under cousins or sons or favourites of the king. In turn, the counties were divided into districts, and the districts sometimes into sub-districts. The smallest independent local group was the village, containing something towards a score of men related to one another by descent from a line of male ancestors, and living with their wives and dependants. Thus this part of Zulu organization was of a type with which we are well familiar: a nation divided into a series of territorial areas of decreasing size. At the centre dwelt the king.

He was the leader of the nation in war, was in command of troops for internal police work, and was supreme judge. He also legislated and took executive action. In addition, he was responsible for carrying out certain ceremonies and for employing magicians in order that the nation might have adequate rains, good crops, freedom from epidemics, and victory in war. For these purposes he also—and he alone—could approach his ancestral spirits who were believed to be partly responsible for the peace and the prosperity of the nation. Finally, he had fields worked by his warriors, and vast herds tended by them; and he drew tribute of cattle and grain from his subjects. This tribute he then mostly redistributed among them. Of course, since the nation occupied some 80,000 square miles and comprised some quarter of a million people he did not exercise these powers himself, but acted through officers; and this meant that considerable power lay in the hands of these officers. Important among them were his county chiefs, and below them their district heads, until at the bottom stood the headmen of villages who ruled over and were responsible for their people.

Here, then, was a simple administrative organization, in which there was delegation of authority from the centre to smaller and then yet smaller local units. This delegation is essential in any administrative system. I repeat, even a tyrant rules through officers; and thus these officers get power. But these Zulu officers drew their power also from another direction. They drew power from the fact that they led the subordinate groups, and represented these to the king who embodied the state. Chiefs, and even headmen, could mobilize armed warriors, so they had fighting power behind them. Herein resided the first of many conflicts which operated inside the apparently simple administrative apparatus. The constitutional position was clear: subordinates were officers of the king and were bound to carry out the king's orders. In practice they also stood for those they ruled against the king himself, and because of this they came into conflict with the king. Certainly they could act to constrain the ways in which the king exercised his power. Thus the village headman not only was responsible to his king, through intermediate officers, for the actions of his villagers, but he also had to represent the interests of his villagers to higher authorities. Similarly, the county chief represented his followers to the king, and was responsible for his followers to the king.

Now, though there was no fundamental cleavage of the Zulu nation into classes differentiated by economic interests, the nature of social interests changed with each step upward in the hierarchy. For example, in this type of nation, the king and the wealthy could not use the produce of land to raise their own standards of living, and so they distributed land to subordinates. The right to land was an attribute of citizenship. Each citizen had an interest in having enough land to support himself and his family, and to build up his own following. But since land varied in fertility and in other qualities, even when the leader was distributing land freely, he had to choose between men. Moreover, a plot of land was not just worked with tools for a living. A plot was worked within a system of social relationships, in which other men had claims on that piece of land or neighbouring land. There were general interests as well as individual interests in each plot. The leader represented these more general interests in land, which were embodied in a code of law controlling land use. If the leader's followers quarrelled over how he distributed the land, or over their holdings or trespasses of stock, he had to judge between them. And in making judgments, whether in administration or in judicial forum, the leader represented the code of law which was liable to restrain various individuals from freely satisfying their desires. The law existed to ensure that all individuals should prosper without trespassing on the claims of others, and this wider interest in security, focused on the leader, might offend individual interest.

The ideals of office required that the leader should be impartial and judge or act without bias, that he be wise in applying the general rules of law justly to the particular circumstances of dispute. Above all, he had to have the courage to take a decision and face the possible dislike, or even anger, of those who lost by his decision. If he failed to act by the ideals of his office, he lost in general repute. But even where he conformed with those ideals he might antagonize some followers. It is important to note that the ideals of office are often contradictory—a king must be just but merciful, generous yet not prodigal, brave but not overbearing. His actions were then doubly exposed since he could be criticized for opposed vices. Over a period of time I observed hostility build up against village headmen and other leaders among the followers they had to restrain and rebuke, even though in particular cases most of their followers approved of their judgments. But this hostility is always there, present in the conflict between sectional interests and group interests represented by the leader.

Men competed for land and goods. Counties competed for land and power inside the nation. In controlling this competition even a fair leader had to restrain someone. Hence Zulu and Barotse explicitly say that when a leader rules he provokes hatred. They go further, and say he provokes hatred when he appears to be doing nothing. Every man, quite naturally, thinks his affairs are all-important. He wants them attended to at once, he cannot see why *he* should wait. The Barotse have a maxim to sum up this egotism of followers: 'Every man thinks that the king has only one subject'.

I have touched here on a series of conflicts which it seems to me must exist in every political system. There are conflicts between the interests of different individuals within a group, and between the interests of smaller groups within a larger society. There is also conflict between society with its law and the individuals and groups which compose society. These conflicts focus on the leaders who have to enforce the law. I am suggesting also that out of the settlement of disputes, or other actions of leaders, there arises hostility against authority which is stated in terms of the first conflict I described—the conflict between the ideals of an office and the human frailty of the incumbent who at any moment occupies that office. Those who are dissatisfied blame neither themselves nor the situation of competing interests. They say the leader is unsatisfactory.

In short, authority may be frail, because human frailty leads the incumbent to fall short of the ideals.

He fails to be an officer and a gentleman, to play a captain's innings, to be a king. But judgments that he has failed may also arise among his followers because he does not appear to take the action which suits them, even when in fact he does live up to the ideal. Clearly these inevitable ideas of shortcomings on the part of leaders will weaken loyalty to them, and even lead to an attempt to overthrow or displace them—to rebellion. In many African tribes, this rebellion is more likely to arise because they have what Sir James Frazer called the Divine Kingship. They believe that there is a mystical connection between the physical and moral well-being of the monarch and the prosperity and success of the tribe. Here then, if there is a drought, or an epidemic among men or cattle, crop-failure or locust swarms, the monarch is held responsible for failing to exhibit the virtues appropriate to his office. The effect of belief in divine kingship is that certain natural misfortunes which overtake any society are blamed on the physical or moral or ritual unworthiness of the king. This is not, of course, purely an African belief. Europeans hold similar beliefs. When the South African Nationalist Party first came to power in 1924, its election propaganda blamed that year's long drought on the moral unworthiness of General Smuts, then Prime Minister. And General Hertzog's first action as Prime Minister was to order a national day of prayer for rain. Rain fell. A British coal crisis, due to vagaries in the weather, may be blamed on the Government in power.

Societies live in complex environments, and leaders are constantly confronted with situations in which they cannot know all the factors involved and have to act on judgment. Moreover, leaders are not normally in full control of any complex situation. Therefore they are always liable to appear to be incompetent, and to provoke rebellion. Under the divine kingship, a leader became liable to attack for failures beyond his control, as well as for weakness, or tyrannical actions and bad judgments or laws. He was attacked if there were what we call natural misfortunes. And this happened though there were no conflicts of class-interest. Other members of the royal family coveted his throne, and were ready to raise rebellion against him. Their excuses for doing so were increased in number by the belief that his personal unworthiness might precipitate national disaster. We have no full score, but certainly legends and historical records of African tribes are full of rebellions.

There are various devices to check attacks on higher authorities. One such obvious device is that in practice, in a large organization, the leader acts through his officers, and it may be possible for him to see that these officers take the blame for shortcomings. That is, they get the unpopularity for misfortunes and bad decisions, while the leader gets the praise for good things. I can illustrate the African rule again from the Barotse of Northern Rhodesia. They hold that the duty of the Prime Minister is to accept responsibility when things go wrong, and to let the king be praised when things go right. I once struck a vivid instance of this in my own entourage. I was trekking with carriers when we ran short of food. The man in charge of my carriers came to ask me how he should reduce their rations. An old Barotse attendant of mine rebuked him: 'You must not tell our lord this. If the carriers know

D

he knows they are short of food they will hate him. You must cut down their food so that they hate you. What do you think he pays you for?' I learnt a valuable lesson from this rebuke. The Barotse capital is in the middle of a treeless flood-plain, and the people are always short of firewood. When I was living there, I had teams of carriers constantly bringing me loads of wood. Inevitably and naturally I was asked for gifts from my store. As a chief should always be generous, even if he goes short himself, it was difficult for me to refuse. So I sent suppliants to beg from my cook, for I said I knew nothing about the firewood. If we were short, my cook would refuse, saying that if he gave any more away, he would not be able to cook my food or provide me with a bath. I could then always say I couldn't override my cook's decision, since by Barotse custom it would be robbing him of his responsibility. But the odium of refusal fell on him. This principle is built deeply into both Barotse and Zulu political rules. The Zulu king Mpande once had to judge on a claim for a large herd of cattle, between the rightful heir who had been born in Swaziland after his father had fled there during the wars of Shaka, and the father's brother who subjected himself to Shaka. The king found in law for the young man, though the uncle, a favourite of his, pleaded that he was being ruined. But the king insisted he had to obey the law. That night he told the uncle he would send a troop to wipe out the young man and his family, so that the uncle would become rightful heir. The king's son heard of this plot and warned the young man, a friend of his. When the prince complained to his father, the king, the reply was that the councillors had hatched the plot of which he was not aware. The Barotse carry this principle to the limit, and insist that their king should not himself take any action, but should always act through his councillors. This enables subjects to sue the councillors if they feel that they are wronged; and the councillors may not plead that they acted on the king's orders. To do so is to commit an offence, 'spoiling the king's name'. Of course, kings frequently did themselves take action, but this provoked severe criticism and in one case a rebellion.

The Barotse use another device, quite consciously, in order to handle this situation of conflict. They state explicitly that it is the lot of leaders to be hated, because they are the Law itself. They say that everyone loves a prince until he is selected to be king: this is why they select him. But as soon as he becomes king everyone hates him—though, of course, they also love him. They apply the same maxim to the smallest authority, down to the village headman, and the father of a family. It was vividly stated for me when I returned to Barotseland in 1947 after an absence of five years. A new king had been elected, who previously had been ruler of an outer province. Many people described to me his installation and recounted the speech he had made. Every one of them recalled, several times, the way the new king said: 'You have brought me here to the capital, from the province where I was happy. You have killed me.' Hatred, then, is won by leadership. But this hatred is diverted partly on to the deputy whom the king appoints to rule for him—the chief councillor. Yet the chief councillor is supposed to represent the people against the king: the Barotse call him 'another kind of king', and he may not be a member of the royal family. But as soon as he is erected into a position of authority to oppose the king, he, too, comes to be the people's enemy, for now he also represents the state. The chief councillor therefore has his own deputy, who has to represent the people against the chief councillor himself. But he, too, becomes an enemy and he has his chief councillor. Thus step by step authority is divided, and some of the hostility of the subjects who are ruled is deflected on to lesser officers.

All officers, up to the king himself, are hence the allies and the enemies of the people they represent, and over whom they rule. The device of delegation of power and deflection of loyalty and hatred controls the working of rebellions, and constrains their direction to maintain the state as a system. For it means that when conflicts do develop into open strife, recalcitrant subjects do not set about destroying the old system itself, but try to raise lower incumbents into higher positions of power; or to alter the personnel entirely. They do not attempt to alter the structure of offices itself. They attack the king they consider tyrannical or weak or an usurper, by turning to their representatives, who are his subordinate officers. In open rebellion, they also turn their opposition into another system of allegiances and loyalties: that of attachment to other princes of the royal family.

I have so far described Zululand as it was organized for administrative purposes into counties and sub-districts, in which county chiefs claimed the loyalty of their followers. But in addition all Zulu were attached separately to princes of the royal family, and if they wanted to rebel against the king they pushed their prince to lead them. The ritual sanctity of the kingship, and its connection with the king's ancestors who presided over national prosperity, meant that if a bad king was to be replaced, he had to be replaced by another member of the royal family. Thus the rebellion attacked the ruling king, but not the kingship itself or the claims of the royal family to it. Princes could lead—or indeed provoke—rebellions without endangering the kingship or their own title to it. We may indeed go further, and say that where the rebellion was against a tyrannical king, the rebels were fighting to defend the kingship, and the values of its office, against the tyrant himself. Rebels were not seeking to establish a different kind of political society, say, a republic, or even to install a different family on the throne. They were seeking to re-establish the kingship in all its ideals, by making a true prince, with the king-becoming graces, into the king.

Of course, princes, and county-chiefs struggling for situations of power around the throne, might provoke these rebellions. It is striking that in African law, as in mediaeval English law, these leaders alone were guilty of treason, and their followers were not. For the followers were under a duty to fight for their chiefs and princes, even against the king.

I think I may safely say that this process was present in all Southern and Central African states. The people had no idea of any kind of political system other than that under which they lived, and there were no cleavages of class-interest to produce revolutions, aiming at a different kind of social order. The conflicts that arose in the nation, over the king's actions and his trespasses on the rights of his subjects, were thus directed by their institutionalized loyalties and allegiances *within* the political system to support kingship and royal family. Over a period of time the cohesion of the system absorbed the conflicts which the system itself set up.

I myself push this analysis a step further. Not all rebellions were waged against kings because they were tyrants. Some princes were ambitious for power, or were pushed by their own officers, seeking for the power that comes from being around the throne, into pursuit of power. They would wage war on the king on the grounds that he was not the rightful king. Or, if the kingship was divine, they would seek the opportunity of a national disaster to attack the kingship on the grounds that the king was ritually unworthy. It seems that these customary beliefs created rebellions. This has led me to think that these rebellions may be necessary to keep the system from breaking into its component parts. The different territorial groups of the Zulu nation tended to develop strong loyalties to their leaders and their own internal autonomy. They came to stand against the kingdom itself. To some extent, the full development of the tendency to separatism was inhibited, because no one county was strong enough to break off and establish itself in its own area on its own. Other counties would support the king against such a rebellion. During the early years of the Zulu kingdom a section on the borders did break out thus. They fought their way to Southern Rhodesia where they formed the Matabele nation. But once the Zulu kingdom was well established, the counties and their chiefs strove for power against one another within the kingdom. But the tendency to separatism seems likely to have persisted. In Zululand there was no integrating economic framework to hold the different sections together; roads and communications were poor in a widely dispersed population. I consider that these tendencies to segment and break up, which resided in the county organization, were offset because of the high, sanctified value of the kingship itself, and because dissatisfaction with the king, arising from county and other local disputes, shifted into allegiances to princes of the royal family. In short, I am suggesting as a problem for investigation—in our own history as well as in Africa—the idea that until a state has an integrated economic system, rebellion against the king, and struggle for the kingship, inhibit the achievement of independence. All sections struggle for the kingship, and this unifies them. They seek to place their own prince on the throne; they do not try to become independent from the kingship. A whole series of customs—the ritual of kingship, the distribution of the royal family, and so forth—produces social order out of the conflicts set up by the same customs. Princes are entitled to be kings: princes struggle for kingship: rebellions reassert the values of kingship and restore its power. The kingship is ritualized: national disaster shows the king to be ritually unworthy: the ritual sacredness of kingship prevents anyone but another prince taking the throne.

I am aware that this is a bold suggestion, and it may seem to be teleological. But in practice when I study the history of African states—or when I read about the Wars of the Roses—it seems clearly to emerge that the effect of rebellion (as against revolution) was at least temporarily to reunite the nation about the kingship. The effect is temporary, for old struggles reassert themselves, and new struggles emerge. But the repetitive process goes on. This central principle, that rebellions attack the personnel of office and not the offices themselves, was stated by Aristotle and is seen by Africans. But it is important to work out the implications of the principle and to trace its operation through connected institutions. Many customs, like beliefs in the divine kingship, thrust conflict and civil war on the nation, and thus produced frequent fights for the desired kingship. For example, there were the rules controlling the selection of heirs to the throne. Rarely in Africa do we find rules which indicate clearly and definitely a single heir. In some kingdoms there was an open free-for-all struggle by princes for the kingship—like the dash for Winchester; in others there was selection by commoner councillors from the princes of the royal family; and in yet others the rules of succession contradicted one another. Or the kingship rotated through different houses of the royal dynasty. Or if the rules themselves were clear, they operated uncertainly in practice. The result was that almost every succession could raise rival claimants, and after the king's death, when national strength was at its weakest, unifying war for the kingship between claimants and their supporters might follow. Strikingly, this conflict of rules, leading to war which in time reunites the nation, did not occur among the Bechuana tribes who dwell concentrated in large towns. Otherwise the very structure of kingship and its rules thrust struggles between rival houses, and even civil war, on the nation; and it is a historical fact that these struggles

kept component sections of the nation united in conflicting allegiance about the sacred kingship. A clearly
marked true heir would not allow competing sections
to put forward equally legitimate claims for the throne.
Early Germanic law had the same conflict of rules of
succession: perhaps a clear legitimist principle with
one heir accompanies only a high degree of local
concentration, or a high degree of economic interdependence between sections of the nation.

I've been trying to describe to you some of the things
which anthropologists have been writing about African
states, and the nature of authority. Of course, I've
selected the points in which I myself am most interested.
They are some of the points which illuminate my main
argument. First, quarrels arise between men because
they live together in society. Secondly, each society has
customs which shape the form which these quarrels
take. But, thirdly, to some extent custom also directs
and controls the quarrels through conflicts of allegiance,
so that despite rebellion, the same social system is
re-established over wider areas of communal life and
through longer periods of time. Indeed, I think this
happens because of rebellion. I don't say the forces
are always perfectly balanced, so that no change
occurs or no state breaks up. We have plenty of
evidence of change and of the break-up of states in
Africa. But these processes work through elaborate
institutional arrangements, which have clearly evolved
through long periods of time; and I am suggesting
only that they inhibit quarrels from destroying the
system: they cannot always prevent that destruction.

So it is clear, to me at any rate, that our studies
show that social life breeds conflict, and societies by

their customary arrangements (which I accept as given) accentuate conflicts. The conflicts in wider ranges compensate one another to produce social cohesion. Nor, may I add, am I suggesting that the resolution of conflicts must always be by force of arms. In Britain we fight periodical civil war on the hustings and in the ballot boxes.

Obviously much of this analysis has already been worked out by the historians and sociologists of our own civilization. Our conclusions fit with theirs. But because we have seen the rebellion principle working in African states where it was not interfered with by economic divisions and the establishment of towns, I think we have been able to push its implications further. And we have seen the rebellion-theme working in more varied forms, than have our historical colleagues. When I go to a Shakespearian historical play I feel that I am back in Africa, sitting at my camp fire, discussing the politics of rebellion with Zulu or Barotse. And when I read the standard works on mediaeval history I do feel that the principle that, in some circumstances, civil war can keep a nation united, might be applied more fully than it is is. Mediaeval states, with their towns and more differentiated economy, were already well past the stage when their civil wars were simple rebellions, without any trace of revolution in them. They were also more fully involved with other states, which interfered in their internal affairs. But the rebellion principle I have outlined for Africa does seem to pull together rules of succession, the law of treason, and other customs, and to explain to some extent the results of civil wars.

These African studies also, I feel, sharpen my reading

of analyses of our modern society, even though this society contains the seeds of revolution as well as constant rebellion. For example, Professor Devons, an economist who worked during the war in the Ministry which planned aircraft production, has pointed out that the variables were so numerous, and many so uncertain, that it was impossible to plan accurately. But the head of the Ministry had to take apparently sensible decisions, though his different production departments swung uneasily between planning for an unattainable target and planning well within capacity. It was the duty of a central directorate to co-ordinate the various plans—to provide the data on which the leader could decide. The whole Ministry was united by a single purpose, the defeat of the Nazis, and it was not divided by major conflicts of interest. Yet Devons says of the central directorate, that there had to be some officials who had no vested interest in any individual programme of production (of engines, propellors, or the like) but an interest only in the finished aircraft programme. These officials had to see there was 'realism in planning'. For example, there was a tendency for sections to conceal their 'fall-downs' in production, and therefore officials were required who had no vested interest in concealment. Here central advice to the leadership emerged. What he goes on to say about this central directorate might apply to a divine king in Africa, thus: 'Although the central directorate had to criticize the plans of the production directorates, it had itself to be above criticism. . . . The prestige of the director- ate, therefore, had to be of the highest order, though it had to be absolved of responsibility. It had also

to be right.' This analysis pin-points the problems of
leadership so strongly, that I am tempted to speak of
the Divine Kingship in the Wartime Ministry of Aircraft Production. And this kingship had its mystical
ritual, for, says Devons, 'The pseudo-scientific atmos-
phere [which] the use of charts and statistics created
gave great power to the statisticians. For it was fairly
easy by the manipulation of statistics and charts to
"prove" a particular case; and the statisticians soon
came to realize that many of the officials not used to
handling figures were both impressed by this manipu-
lative power and incapable of acquiring it themselves.'
Perhaps no divine king has wielded a more powerful
or esoteric ritual.

Devons's study makes quite clearly all the points
about the alteration in the interests influencing men at
different levels of an hierarchical system, and shows
how these are controlled, again, in a system not
divided by obvious clashes of interest.

Here, as even in the undifferentiated economies of
Africa, there is conflict about the leader's position—
his two-way representation of different kinds of interest,
for instance. Hence we should expect sharpening of
the conflict in our industrial and political system,
which contains many competing economic and other
interests. For example, our industrial relations are
now largely adjusted through highly developed,
institutional, negotiating machinery. In this machinery
trade union leaders, whatever party is in power, have
an important rôle. They have, in effect, largely become
part of the governmental and management systems for
mobilizing and paying labour; therefore they have to
represent the wider interests of state and productive

industry, as well as the narrower interests of their own followers. Deep conflicts about their position are set up, which are not being compensated for within institutional arrangements. One result is the throwing up from the ranks, by the workers, of unofficial leaders who represent the interests of workers alone, without the competing influence of wider national interests. The fact that many strikes are declared by trade union leaders to be 'unofficial' is another symptom of this situation of unresolved authority-conflict.

In Central Africa, we have studied the similar situation of the village headman. Here is the man who moves among the subjects and who is involved in their day-to-day difficulties and struggles; yet who has to represent the state against them—he sees they pay their taxes and perform state-labour, he reports them if they break the law, and so forth. Thus the village headman in most tribes is the centre of a constant struggle, both in terms of backbiting and intrigue, and of a war in the mystical world. For he is believed to attain his position and maintain it by using witchcraft against his rivals; and he himself constantly suspects that he is the target of the envious witchcraft of his rivals, and of those whom he has rebuked. Among the Barotse, I remember a headman who kept tapping an ulcer on his face and saying, 'It's the government, it's the government, it's the government'—meaning that because of his position under the government he had been bewitched with the ulcer. These beliefs indicate the strong conflicts which are operating about the headman's position. I suggest that this is because he is the man at the bottom of the state hierarchy, who most directly represents the state to his subordinates, and yet who is moving among them and immediately subject to the pressure of their interests. He takes the greatest strain of the conflict between the dual pulls of political representation. To-day, in Central Africa, a similar position is occupied by the African chief in relation to the Colonial Government. He is an officer of that Government and should represent its interests and values to the African people; and yet he should stand on his people's behalf for the values and interests which they esteem. The chief thus takes on his shoulders the conflict between the authority of the Colonial Government, and the aspirations of his own people—as seems to have happened with the Kabaka of Buganda.

The position of the lowermost man in an hierarchical system can be traced in situation after situation. There are the foreman and the charge-hand, who have on behalf of management to supervise the workers who are their fellows. They are management, but not quite enough to be called 'Mister'. Hence there is to-day in Britain considerable debate about the position of the foreman, as there is about the shop steward. Nowadays the shop steward, the lowest-ranking official in the trade union hierarchy, frequently appears as an agitating trouble-maker. For he is the man at the bottom of the system who is responsible to his superiors, representing wider interests, and yet he is also the man who works and lives with those who are organized and administered. He feels the constant pressure of their interests, and these may force him into conflict with higher trade union officials as well as with management. Hence the shop steward bears the brunt of much of the conflict between the interests of workers and the wider interests of the nation. I see him as taking the full weight of the resentment against the controlling administration as such. The frailty of conflicting authority is strong in him. And if in him, perhaps also in the non-commissioned officer, the hospital ward-sister, and the poor school prefect.

III

ESTRANGEMENT IN THE FAMILY

ANYONE reading a book about an African society must be struck with the number of special customs and taboos which attach to the relations between spouses, and between parents and their children. African domestic life, in anthropological summaries, seems to be full of special observances, and of ceremonies to mark the advancement of individuals from birth, through weaning and puberty, to maturity and old age. These customs and taboos serve to mark out marital and parental relationships. In many tribes marital intercourse is fraught with mystical danger and has to be approached with ritual safeguards, while casual liaisons occur without customary inhibition. When a wife is pregnant, she has to avoid many mystical threats; she herself may be dangerous to things virile. In all tribes, when she is menstruating she is full of this mystical danger. From early infancy girls taboo certain foods to protect their future children. A mother's milk has sometimes to be cleansed of ritual impurity before her child can drink it. Thus marital and maternal functions are given a cultural distinctiveness over and above their organic basis. The biological distinctions between wife and husband, and between mother and father, are accentuated by custom.

Custom similarly accentuates the difference between

parents and children. A Bechuana father's or mother's anger against a wayward child is more than disciplinary: it carries a mystical curse. Among the Tallensi of the Gold Coast, a man's first-born son and daughter may not eat the domestic fowl, may not wear any of their father's garments or his quiver, and may not look into his granary during his lifetime. A man and his eldest son do not eat together. A woman's first-born daughter may not uncover her mother's chief storage-pot. A Tsonga youth or maiden must not mention sexual or even marital affairs to parents, but keeps them informed through intermediaries. And so it goes on. The details of custom and taboo and mystical fear may vary, but there is this constant general difference between African domestic relations and our own—in Africa there is a whole series of rules to regularize relations within the family. And it is striking that while on the one hand the members of the family are brought together by these rules, on the other hand they are forced apart and estranged from one another. The customs exhibit conflict and estrangement, as well as co-operation and kinship of interest. This evening I am going to discuss how these estrangements within the African family are related to the cohesion of the larger society.

Difficulties between spouses, and between parents and children, are not, of course, peculiar to African society. But in Britain we consider that they should not occur, that family life should be loving and harmonious. And our culture does not itself state in its customs that these conflicts in the family are inevitable—indeed, they don't exist in many families. Neither do they exist in many African families, for

E

there, too, the ideal is love and harmony. But African customs state that conflicts are inevitably present within this harmony. In his study of *The Web of Kinship among the Tallensi*, Professor Fortes has a chapter entitled 'Tensions in the Parent-Child Relationship'. He begins it with this revealing statement: 'Perhaps the most extraordinary feature of Tallensi parents' relations with their children is the recognition, in custom and belief, of the latent antagonism behind their mutual identification and comradeship, their devotion and co-operation'. . . . 'A psycho-analyst might say', Fortes goes on, 'that the Œdipus complex is apparently openly recognized in Tallensi culture. He would have to add that the Œdipus complex is built into their social organization in such a way as to enable them to control it. The mystical ideas and ritual symbols in which the rivalry between successive generations is clothed form the cultural mechanism by which it is neutralized and made to serve socially useful ends.'

Fortes points out that the 'superficial symbolism' of the taboo between a man and his oldest son is 'transparent. What they mean is that a child may not be equated with his or her father while he is alive.' I myself think we may seek the reason for this open expression of competition between father and son, in the limited economic and political opportunities which are open to men in these subsistence societies. In modern Britain, a man grows out of his dependence on his parents into a large-scale society containing many differentiated functional groups. He does not have to compete directly with his father for the means of livelihood, and for control of property. In addition, he does not have to compete with his father for a wife, as he may have to do in a society which allows polygamy, so that elderly men can still be marrying young women. Similarly, brothers have to compete among themselves directly for limited land and stock, for the means to marry, and for opportunities for political advancement. Hence there is open rivalry, stated in custom, between brothers. But I don't consider that these social limitations are the only reason why in Africa custom so openly emphasizes differences between the various members of the family. I think the taboos are also important because they introduce divisions—estrangements—into the family and prevent it absorbing the whole-hearted emotional allegiance of its members. Husbands are forced apart from their wives to continued association with their own kin, and children turn to more distant kin and away from their parents. The estrangements in the family are associated with the extension of ties to wider kinship groupings. These groupings support the family, but they are also inimical to the family. And they are important in building the cohesion of the larger society. This is what I described in discussing the peace of the feud. Wider kinship links establish interwoven webs of kinship which unite men in allegiances, often backed by mystical sanctions, over a large area. This is their political importance. The links are economically important in that they provide aid in productive tasks and safeguards against natural disasters which always threaten groups living not much above subsistence.

The family of father, mother, and children is an important group in practically all societies. Mating of the sexes is necessary for the physical continuity of the society, and this mating is always controlled by cultural rules which regularize relations. In addition, it is largely in the family that cultural continuity, the handing on of the social heritage, is accomplished, since parents train their children in the culture of their society. But in modern urban industrial society the family in this way, with the help of schools and other agencies, produces recruits for specialized functional groups—factories, political associations, churches, clubs, and the like. These are on the whole groups united by a single interest. Only when the children grow up and marry do relations in the one family come into conflict with the pulls of another kinship group: a new family, with intensive emotional attachments involving a whole series of interests. African society lacks such functional single-interest groups: its technology is not adequate to support these. The larger groups of African society also are kinship groups, which involve high sentimental attachment: and hence they have to draw the members of various families together, by driving wedges into the family itself. Custom and taboo and ceremony drive these wedges; other customs link the members of several families into the larger kinship system; and there are varying customs to demarcate the different kinds of kinsfolk.

I think that no anthropologist has yet explicitly stated the conflict between the interests of the family and the interests of the wider kinship groupings, as a general theoretical proposition, or examined the significance of customary rules in the light of this proposition. But it has been used in a number of specific studies. For example, among the Nuer the larger political structure consists of extended groups of men linked to one another by descent through males. Here, says Professor Evans-Pritchard, certain forms of mating between the sexes strengthen 'sentiments of kinship, because there is in these cases no single undivided family . . . to demand a man's major allegiance at the expense of the solidarity of the wider kinship group which provides a boy with scope for his deepest interests and ambitions'. This implies that the family itself demands allegiance *at the expense* of the wider kinship group—and obviously also that the wider kinship group demands allegiance at the expense of the family. Elsewhere in his analysis, Evans-Pritchard uses the phrase, 'subordinating the rôles of the family and of the father to the interests of the wider groups of paternal kin and the lineage'.

Here is recognition of the conflict between parental and filial allegiances, and wider kinship allegiances. The same pulls affect marital allegiances. Professor Schapera summed up Bechuana marital relations with ironic moderation: 'There is a general absence of enthusiastic co-operation between husband and wife'. He refers this attitude to several social factors, such as polygamous marriages, the separation of the sexes in social life, and so forth. Then he goes on: 'From the wife's point of view, the happiness of her marriage sometimes depends not so much upon her husband himself as upon his parents and other relatives among whom she is living. While she generally manages to get on fairly well with them, it happens now and then that they grow jealous of her and begin to dislike her, especially if they feel that her husband is devoting all his attention to her and is not supporting them as liberally as before. They will then start grumbling, possibly with justice, that she is lazy, disobedient, or flighty in her conduct; they will continually run down her family; and if her husband takes her part will accuse her and her parents of having won him over by the use of love-potions. She, on the other hand, may have cause for complaint in the burdens they thrust upon her, and in their attempts to restrict her from visiting or entertaining her friends; and should she still be childless after a few years, she will readily attribute this to their evil dispositions or their use of sorcery. Occasionally, if she finds life with them particularly difficult, she may even persuade her husband to come and live with her permanently at the home of her parents.' Now this sort of situation, in which one spouse's parents are jealous of the other spouse's demands on their child, is not unknown among ourselves. But among the Bechuana it is institutional-ized in the belief that love-potions may be used by the wife and her parents to gain her husband's full atten-tions, against the conventional requirements that a man should continue after marriage to spend his time with his kinsmen and his wealth in their support. If a man is too devoted to his wife, Barotse and Bemba say that she has bewitched him out of his senses; much as we still say that a woman can bewitch a man's senses. And the African wife fears the sorcery of her relatives-in-law, as they fear hers.

I am interested, as throughout these lectures, in the extent to which African custom emphasizes the conflicts between a man's or a woman's interests and allegiances. The customs I am discussing this evening also emphasize the specific rôles of each member of the family. A woman's femininity is enhanced by menstrual and pregnancy taboos: menstruation and pregnancy are made into more than physiological functions. Their threat to her husband's virility and health mark her separation from him. The ideas of impurity and ritual danger, and yet of a fertility which can be conveyed to crops, which are believed to be present in marital relations, raise these relations from the purely physical. These customs and taboos extend their influence throughout the relations of spouses. In Central Africa, a man is not allowed to cook when he is in the village, though he may cook on a journey: in the village, every man is dependent on some woman to cook for him. This cultural exaggeration of the different, complementary rôles of spouses and their children is also present in the whole kinship system. Divisions in the family are related to divisions in the wider society.

African kinship systems vary considerably from one another, but their widespread extension always involves the grouping of more distant kin with close kin. For instance, some years ago a Ganda, Akiki Nyabongo, dedicated his book, *Africa Answers Back*, 'To My Mothers'—in the plural. He told me that the publishers altered the dedication to the singular, 'mother'; but he insisted on reinstating the plural. For a man in an African tribe calls many women 'my mother', though he knows quite well who his own mother is, and she is closest to him. But if his father has several wives, they all rank as 'mother' to him, and their children are his brothers and sisters. The wives of his father's brothers and paternal cousins are similarly 'mothers' to him. On the other side, his mother's sisters are also 'mothers', and so are some of her cousins. In some tribes, this extension of the term 'mother' may be carried so far as to override sexual distinctions: a man can appear to count in some ways as a woman, and a woman appears to count as a man. Most notably, this appears in the position of the mother's brother, who is grouped with his sister and called 'male-mother'. Once when I was working in Barotseland during the war, a new District Commissioner told me that he had had an inquiry from the Army about a Barotse soldier who had overstayed his leave. The soldier's excuse was that while he was at home his mother had died, and he had stayed for her funeral. The District Commissioner had found that it was the soldier's mother's brother who had died. I explained that the Barotse call the mother's brother 'my male-mother', or more simply even 'my mother'. The mother's brother was a very close relative whose funeral a man should attend. So the District Commissioner wrote to the Army: 'Please ask the soldier if his mother was a woman or a man. If he says his mother was a woman, he is lying; if he says his mother was a man, he is telling the truth.'

By grouping the mother's brother with the mother these tribes are asserting that he owes to his sister's child affectionate support and care which are not compelled as a matter of legal right, but given out of generosity and love. In a patriarchal society where property passes from father to son, and groups of men thus related are linked by corporate legal interests, there is what Evans-Pritchard calls 'a hardness' in their relations. The maternal line, on the other hand, is not dominated by these legal considerations. It serves, as I showed in discussing the peace of the feud, to break into the hard loyalty of agnatic groups related through males, and to spread links of sentimental interest throughout the society. Hence in many patriarchal societies a boy acquires his social individuality from his maternal links. He is tied to his paternal kin by strong interests in property held in common. There are rivalries over this property. He begins to build up his own personal estate from small stock given to him by his mother's brother. And the sanctions in this line of descent are moral and ritual, rather than legal. A mother's brother's curse may be the most dreadful a man can face; and in some tribes a sister's son has similar powers to afflict his uncle. The maternal line in some of these patriarchal societies is thus seen as carrying a mystical threat to the welfare and solidarity of the paternal group. For they believe that it is in this line that the dreadful power of witchcraft may be inherited. Among the Tsonga of Mozambique and the Tallensi of the Gold Coast, witchcraft passes like haemophylia: from women to their children, so that men can carry it, but not transmit it. Stranger women bring witchcraft into the group of men, and their daughters take it out again.

In these patriarchal societies, as the mother's brother is grouped with the mother, so the father's sister may be grouped with the father. Like the father's brothers, she is a father—literally, she may be called 'female-father'. This entails showing respect to her as to the father, while the mother's sister is treated with the same easy tenderness as the mother.

But in societies where succession to office and inheritance of property are not from father to son, but from

mother's brother to sister's son—what we call matrilineal societies—the legal position is reversed. Here
legal rights, with their hardness, exist in the matrilineal
line; and the father and his kin support a man with
love and solicitude unmarred by the ambivalence
which arises from conflicts over property.

I have here sketched in outline, without any of the
complicating variations found in different tribes, one
of the principles which underlie an extended kinship
system. I am not going to examine other principles,
by which various sorts of kin are grouped with brothers
and sisters and children, or different kinds of cousins
are distinguished, or grandparents and grandchildren
are identified with one another. This is an intricate
and fascinating field of study—through the work of
Professor Radcliffe-Brown, the doyen of anthropology,
this aspect of kinship systems forms probably the most
considerable body of systematic knowledge which we
have. The conflicts which exist in these systems do
indeed illustrate my main thesis, for they balance and
redress one another to produce cohesion in the wider
society. But I am here chiefly concerned with estrangements inside the family, estrangements caused by the
extended kinship system, and I am going to exhibit
their cohesive effect in one instance by examining the
relations of spouses.

All societies require children if they are to continue
physically; and women produce the children by mating
with men. It would be sufficient for organic reproduction if this mating with men was casual, as it is among
animals. But the period of human gestation is long, it is
incapacitating to women as it is not to female animals,
and the human baby is helpless for a long period.

Beyond this, the baby has to be taught language, trained in the use of tools, and given a vast cultural apparatus. Language, tools, and the cultural apparatus of a society exist independently of any one individual: they endure through the passing of the generations. Culture has to be transmitted from one generation to another. This is one important function of the family, the bringing-up of the baby to maturity within a particular culture. But the cultural apparatus of a society is not held indiscriminately and equally by all its members. Some individuals have more skills than others, more power, esoteric knowledge, and ritual. And property is divided in different lots, and often in different arrangements and amounts, between the members of a society. Therefore every society provides both for a general transmission of culture—language and ideas, tools, customs—to the new generation; and also for the transmission of particular items of culture and of property from certain members of the senior generation to certain members of the junior generation.

It is also significant that in those African societies where there is little utilitarian property, men of high position own ritual symbols which strengthen that position. For succession in all systems involves not only orderly transmission of property, but also orderly maintenance of an established arrangement of social relations between a large number of people: when a man dies, the structure of social relations is maintained by substituting another for him. 'The king is dead, long live the king.' Once we are dealing with the continuance of society through generations, we are involved in far more complex problems than those of simple organic continuity. Organically the closest link between old and new generations is that between mother and child. But in, I think, every society of which we have accurate knowledge, power and property belong principally to men, and younger men succeed to their seniors' powers and positions and goods. In some instances, heirs are chosen by selection or election; but a large part of succession and inheritance is by descent.

The persistence of a social structure involves the replacement of a dead man by an heir. As this appears in individual life, a man has to have heirs. But he can only get heirs of a younger generation through a woman. Here is a major conflict in the family and kinship system: women produce children, play the larger part in organic transmission; but social transmission of property and position is largely from man to man. So that men depend on women for social perpetuation. Under patrilineal father-right a man depends on his wife. Under matrilineal mother-right he depends on his sister. And in some societies, a man may get his heirs through both his wife and his sister. The simple organic facts of perpetuation are complicated by the transmitting of social as well as organic endowment through women.

There are in every African society elaborate rules defining the women whom a man can and cannot marry. As universally, there is a strong taboo on marriage within the family. Parents and children are never allowed to marry: only in a few royal families can the king marry a sister, and this is usually his half-sister by his father, and not his full-sister by mother and father. Commoners must seek for spouses outside

their natal family; and the taboo on sexual relations
with own parents and sister may be widely extended
to more distant kinswomen. The historical origin of
this taboo on incest is buried deep in time. There has
been considerable speculation about how it arose, but
anthropologists now accept it as so constant a part of
human relations, that we take it as something without
which society could not exist—much, I suppose, as
we cannot conceive of the physical universe without
gravity.

Transmission of the social heritage therefore proceeds
through mating in which men are not allowed to
breed on their own sisters, and sometimes other
kinswomen. The situation seems simplest in matrilineal societies, where succession to office and inheritance is from a woman's brother to her son. This type
of succession—the linking of a man to his sister and
then her son—may be widely extended, and large
kinship groups may be built up by the principle.
This is the position, for instance, among the Ashanti of
the Gold Coast, and through large areas of Central
Africa. Here a man is socially reproduced, so to
speak, not in his own son, but in his nephew by his
sister. He is responsible for his sister's well-being and
his nephew inherits his property and position. But
though his sister provides him with his heir, he may
not, under the ban on incest, himself beget her children.
He has to get some other man, or men, to cohabit
with his sister in order that she have children, some of
whom will be his heirs and successors. Theoretically,
I suppose it would be possible for a group of brothers
to work their lands together and keep their sisters
around them, while other men visited the sisters in

fleeting liaisons and provided children to continue the resident matrilineal group. In practice, this situation, in which the women are visited by completely chance men, is not found anywhere. On the contrary, even in matrilineal systems, there are rules to control the mating of the sexes, and with very few exceptions there is stressing of the rôle of some man as father. A woman should have an accredited husband to be father to her children: Malinowski called this 'the principle of legitimacy'. Fathers have important psychical and social rôles in the development of their sons and their daughters. And marriage itself is strengthened by customary rules till it involves more than just sexual and procreative relations: it is not simple complementary biological co-operation. Here the taboos on a man's cooking, and the ritual value attached to marital intercourse, are significant in widening the ties of marriage. As Durkheim indicated, the social exaggeration of male and female rôles, by dividing men from women more sharply, strengthens marriage bonds.

But there is, in matrilineal societies, considerable variation in the degree to which the father's rôle is stressed. It tends to be less where the woman after marriage resides with her brother, and her husband comes to live in their house, or to visit her. If the husband takes his wife to his home, even though their children will succeed to his brother-in-law, the husband's rôle as father is likely to be more important. In all African matrilineal societies which have been studied, the father's rôle is marked. The father's rôle seems to have been reduced to a minimum among the Nayar castes of Malabar in India in the past.

The Nayar kinship grouping was a matrilineal lineage living on its own property. Sisters remained in their brothers' house. Nayar women might have several 'lovers' of their own caste, or higher castes, and each man might have several 'mistresses'. There has been dispute over whether marriage existed here. But Dr. Kathleen Gough has made clear that there was social control of fatherhood. In the first place, all Nayar women were married before puberty to men of their own caste, and divorced after four days; so that their children had the right caste, as a whole, for 'father'. Pollution taboos were observed by all a woman's children, by whomsoever they were begotten, on the death of their mother's ritual husband, since he ranked as their ritual father. Secondly, a woman was forbidden to have relations with men of inferior caste. Thirdly, her brothers exercised control over the men who visited her in their home; they could object to her taking as a lover a man of whom they did not approve. And all of a woman's lovers had to make gifts to her at the birth of a child and at certain festivals. But women and men were constantly changing their lovers. The Nayars afford the extreme example of a matrilineal system with a very weak conjugal bond; but even among them, the conjugal bond, and fatherhood, were socially instituted and ritualized.

Yet we see clearly in this extreme form of the matrilineal system, where sisters did not leave their brothers' houses, something typical of all matrilineal systems. In these systems the bond of a woman to her brother, whose heir she will produce, is strong. On the other hand, her bond to the man with whom she cohabits and who begets her children is weak. In fact, I might say she has weak bonds with the series of men with whom she cohabits: for it is characteristic of African matrilineal systems, and of those in other lands, that where a woman remains in her natal home the marriage bond is fragile and the divorce rate is high.

Patrilineal systems, where sons succeed to their father, inherit his property, and become primarily members of his group, present the opposite situation. Here the woman is moved out of her natal family in order to produce children for her husband and his line. Therefore the bonds which tie a woman to her husband are extremely strong, and her bonds with her brother are weakened by her marriage: the divorce rate is low. Indeed, among the patriarchal peoples of South and North-east Africa (as in India and in Rome in the earliest days), there is virtually no divorce. But the basic principle in building up these patrilineal systems, in which property passes from a man to his son, is still the link of mother to child. Here the principle is that the children of a woman belong by law to her husband: thus *pater est quem nuptiae demonstrant* was the Roman Law rule. 'The father is indicated by the marriage ceremony.' In large areas of Africa this demonstration is achieved by a man's paying cattle for his bride. This payment gives a man rights in his bride's child-bearing capacity; and once a man has given cattle for a woman all her children are his, whosoever the physiological father may be. In some tribes, in the rare event of a divorce all the former husband's cattle are returned to him and his children belong to the new husband who pays another lot of cattle to her kin. Or if a woman has had illegitimate children, when a man pays cattle for her at marriage he obtains these children even though he did not beget them. Adulterine children belong to the husband, and their begetter cannot claim them.

The bond established by this payment of cattle is so strong that it is not broken even by the death of the husband. He remains married to his wife, even though he is dead. A kinsman is chosen by the widow, or selected by his kin, to cohabit with her, and the dead husband still ranks as father to the children, though he could not beget them. This institution can produce what to us are curious results. Professor Schapera reports from the Bechuana that when a man dies and leaves several wives, his son by one wife may cohabit with one of the other widows. He may then beget a boy who is physiologically his son, but whom he will call 'brother'. Physiological paternity is neglected. Similarly, in some of these societies when a wife dies her kin may send a sister to step into her place and continue the marriage.

In these institutions physiological paternity is distinguished from social fatherhood—as anthropologists put it, the *pater* need not be the *genitor*. A man can become pater to children conceived after his death. Indeed, among South and North-east African tribes, a man may become a father though he dies before marriage. Out of family pride, or to avoid misfortune from his perturbéd spirit, his kinsmen may marry a wife to his name, and she will bear children for him. The children are his because the cattle given for the bride are given in his name, and therefore, though dead, he is her husband. And, under this rule, a woman who has cattle can marry another woman, and be pater to her children begotten by some man. Women

F

who act thus are often barren, but sometimes a female husband is herself married as a woman and is mother to her own children, while she is pater to other children. Thus in South-east Africa, if a man has died leaving daughters and cattle, but no sons, the chief may order the eldest daughter to act in this way, as if she were a man, in order to continue her father's line.

These varieties of marriage in patriarchal societies all exhibit a stability which is impervious not only to divorce but also to death. The central legal rule is that the payment of cattle links a woman strongly to a man, even if he is dead; and this husband, though incapable of begetting children, is the father to all her children. The Roman Law maxim, that the pater is indicated by the marriage-ceremonies, among the Zulu is stated as, *izinkomo zizala abantwana*—'cattle beget children'. But cattle beget children by binding a woman to a man, her husband. Hence, in patriarchal as in matrilineal societies, the primary link is of mother to child. Professor Evans-Pritchard states this principle for the Nuer, thus: 'The social principle of agnatic descent is, by a kind of paradox, traced through the mother, for the rule is that in virtue of the payment of cattle all who are born of the mother are children of the husband'. The Nuer are an egalitarian people, without rank. Dr. Hilda Kuper studied the Swazi of South Africa, a highly ranked society; and there the rule emerged even more strongly. She writes that 'the fundamental principle underlying the selection of an heir is that power is inherited from men, and acquired by them; but it is transmitted through women, whose rank, more than any single factor, determines the choice of the successor'. That is, when Swazi select an heir to a dead man who had had several wives, the mother of the heir is the wife of highest rank. Hence, say the Swazi, 'a ruler is ruler by his mother', though he succeeds to the position of his father.

Thus the two contrasting types of kinship system, extreme father-right and extreme matriliny, are built up on the same principle: the link of mother to child. The child is linked to men through its mother, and not directly. But the two different ways of linking the mother to men, to her husband or to her brother, have very different effects on the internal structure of the family, and the relations between spouses and their children. In both forms they are estranged from one another by the pull in different directions of the larger kinship groups.

I am suggesting in this analysis that as the organic facts of mating and procreation are socialized within an extended kinship system, a fundamental conflict centres on the position of the woman. This conflict is clearly expressed in the separation from one another of different kinds of rights in a woman which may be held by different men—primarily by her natal kin, and by her husband. When I say rights in a woman are held by men, I do not mean that she is a slave. This she certainly is not. She has her own rights, and the men who hold rights over her owe her important obligations. But these rights are held by men. The two main rights in a woman are: firstly, rights in her as a wife; and secondly, rights in her as a child-bearer.

What happens in a matrilineal society is that these two rights are separated and are held by different sets of men. The woman's kin transfer to the husband, often in return for gifts, rights in her as a wife. Under the rules prohibiting incest they cannot themselves exercise these rights. They retain rights in her, and owe her duties, as a daughter, sister, aunt, and so on; and they also retain rights in her as a child-bearer. Her children primarily strengthen their line. In patriarchal societies the woman's kin transfer to her husband rights in her both as a wife and as a child-bearer. It seems to be the second set of rights, over a woman's child-bearing capacity, which established the firmer relationship. Hence in matrilineal societies where she bears children mainly for her own blood-kin, her wifely bond is weak. Divorce is frequent; women are liable to side with their brothers against their husbands. A man trusts his sister, and not his wife: 'Your sister is always your sister; to-morrow your wife may be another man's wife'. In the patriarchal society where she bears children for her husband's group, her wifely bond is strong, enduring perhaps beyond death.

In these different ways the extended kinship system pulls on the spouses and separates them from one another. The conflict of the opposed pulls is primarily on the woman, and the conflict of allegiances centres on her. The pull is primarily on her, because of the nature of her contribution to organic reproduction: she carries the baby within herself for a long period and then she suckles, nurses, and rears it. Physiologically, the male contribution can be short and ephemeral. In the extreme matrilineal systems, therefore, a woman can be changing her husband frequently, while the natal bond with her brother remains strong. In the patriarchal systems, since men cannot marry their sisters they must marry stranger-women to get children. A man marries a woman and brings her to his group:

he begets a child whom she rears under his protection, and then she conceives another child. The woman is firmly bound to her husband, divorce is rare, her bonds with her brother are weakened. Divorce may not be allowed whatever the personal relations of the spouses. Kuper reported a case from the Swazi where a man nearly beat his wife to death. The Swazi judges said they could not divorce her, but they also could not allow her to live with her husband who would kill her: she should live with her brother and seek lovers whose children would belong to her husband.

It is obvious how in a matrilineal system the pulls of inheritance and succession rights on a woman and her children estrange her from her husband. But generally ties with the husband's kin are also effective, and these attachments produce divisions in the loyalties of individuals and lead them into relationship with other sets of people. One of the main pulls away from the one-sided strength of the matrilineal group is the attachment of the woman to her husband, and of the children to their father. Despite the frequency of divorce, marriage in these societies is not merely a means whereby a woman gets a sexual partner who will beget children for her line. In the patriarchal systems, it is the strength of the husband's ties with his kin which draw him away from his wife. As I quoted from Schapera, the man who devotes too much attention to his wife, and allows himself to concentrate on her and his children, provokes resentment from his kin which may be expressed in beliefs in sorcery. Meanwhile the wife remains attached by sentiment, supported by custom, to her own kin, and thus draws her children into relationship with them. Even though divorce is rare in these patriarchal societies, the spouses are estranged from one another by the pulls of their natal kin.

Each of the spouses has to maintain strong links with his or her own kin, and these links are often supported by mystical penalties. This is the conventional mode of behaviour. There is no expectation of intensive emotional attachments between spouses. Dr. Audrey Richards, writing about marriage among the Bemba of Northern Rhodesia, says: 'I once amazed a group of elderly Bemba by telling them an English folk-tale about the difficulties experienced by a prince in winning the hand of his bride—glassy mountains, chasms, dragons, giants and the like. An old chief present was genuinely astonished: "Why not take another girl?" he said.' A similar attitude was shown by some Fingo elders who were discussing the problem of increasing runaway marriages and illegitimate births with the 1883 Commission on Native Law and Custom in South Africa. One of them complained: 'It is all this thing called love. We do not understand it at all. This thing called love has been introduced.' If husband and wife are so devoted to one another, or jealous of one another, that they insist against convention on spending their time together, then it is commonly thought that the woman has used magic to win her husband's love. But in most cases spouses observe the conventions and do not spend too much time in one another's company, nor neglect their kin. It is custom which emphasizes their estrangement, whatever the actual nature of their personal relations. Similarly, many parents and children are devoted to one another, even though custom insists that they must exhibit signs of rivalry and tension. In our own society the converse is true: custom and convention ask for the exhibition of harmony between all members of the family, even if in practice many families are full of rivalry and discord.

I don't want you to think that African spouses do not have strong attachments, companionship, passion, and love. They do indeed. But the attachment between spouses, with its potentially high emotional involvement, has to compete in the individual's sentimental life with wider attachments to other kin. People live in villages with their kinsmen and kinswomen; spouses are not isolated in separated houses. From infancy their children are constantly dealing with relatives who stand to them as substitutes for parents and brothers and sisters, or who may have special duties towards them. The general effect is that the child grows up with many affectionate relatives, to whom he builds up sentimental attachments, even if these are not as close as his attachments to his own parents. But the conflicts in these relationships may also be less. When he is annoyed with his own parents he can seek refuge with these others; if he is orphaned, they partially take his parents' place. These distant kin are organized in property-holding groups which co-operate in many activities, and in which he has to seek to fulfil his own social development. This organization of groups pulls him out of the family, estranging him from too solid an allegiance to it, and leading him into relation with more distant kin.

The general effect of this sort of kinship situation seems to be a dispersal of attachments, which may well be reflected in the relationship of spouses, so that emotional bonds in marriage do not outweigh other ties. There is a marked conventional division of labour between men and women, and the society disbelieves in platonic relationships between them. Men work and spend their leisure time with men, women with women. One observer has said that a man seeks companionship with other men, loves his sister, and sleeps with his wife. This is an exaggeration; but it stresses the need to examine family relations in the light of wider social relationships. The whole situation, in these societies with few specialized skills and large subsistence group-ings, accords with the importance of building up net-works of individual ties of interest with many kin. Customary restrictions on the relations of a man with his kinswomen force him into intimate conjugal relationship with a stranger woman, and this brings him to associate with other men and groups. Customary restrictions on the extent of his intimacy with his wife maintain his ties with his natal kin. The wife is similarly placed. Divisions within the family are associated with the wider bonds of kinship. The estrangements in the family are part of the cohesion of the larger society.

The situation in certain families in Western Europe may not be entirely different from this. We tend to think always of a more isolated and exclusive elemen-tary family, living on its own, with intensive conjugal, parental and filial ties. Yet apparently the same processes as I've described for Africa are operating here. An uncompleted study by Miss Elizabeth Bott of a few British urban familes suggests that where a family has scattered ties with relatives, neighbours, friends, and workmates, the spouses act much more together. But where relatives, neighbours, friends, and workmates tend to be the same people (as they are in Africa), the activities of spouses become separated. This is certainly the position in long-settled rural areas. In some villages, men and women are organized as separate groups, largely opposed to one another. A widespread set of relationships with relatives seems to involve the splitting of the elementary family. Where it is isolated from its kin, the family's members are thrown together. Therefore, nowadays, as African families move into the new towns, away from their kin, the conjugal bond becomes more intense.

I have concentrated my analysis of the African family on the relations of spouses, and how these are influenced by the wider kinship system. I described how it is possible to separate the rôles of a married woman into wife and child-bearer. Where she bears children for a group other than that of her husband, she is pulled away from her husband and the divorce-rate is high. Where she bears children for the man to whom she is wife, she is firmly bound to him. Though in the European family a woman's rôles are not split thus, it doesn't mean that the understanding we gain from African studies, has no significance for our own family problems. If this hypothesis of the connection between divorce-rates and the type of extended kinship system is correct, it affords in another sphere a validation of the sociological argument that social factors and not only personal disharmonies may control divorce-rates in Western society. There are here many complicating factors, such as religious bans on divorce, costs of divorce, the existence of legal separation as well as divorce, and the like.

But the decline of father-right and extensive property rights may be at work weakening the family.

We learn something more. It is commonly said that the family is the basis of society, and anthropological evidence tends to confirm this moral judgment. But it may not be one unbroken family. For matrilineal societies have undoubtedly persisted for many generations in their present forms, with considerable instability in marital relations. But these societies do have considerable stability, which exists in the extended kinship groupings and in other long-enduring groups, for which the unstable families provide recruits. It therefore appears to me—I throw this out as a suggestion—that it might be profitable to approach the problem of divorce in Western society by examining the relation between the individual family and the larger and enduring social groups for which the family breeds new recruits. These groups are functional groups, and not kinship groups. The organization of our society in these functional groups appears to allow the individual family to exist without custom-induced estrangement.

IV

THE LOGIC IN WITCHCRAFT

IN the year 1831 Nathaniel Isaacs, a young member of the first party of English traders to settle among the Zulu of Natal, made the following entry in his diary: 'A body of people in the neighbourhood came to us with pensive looks and complaining in a pitiful strain that sickness had invaded their families. They seemed to think it singular that they alone should be sick while all the people around them were enjoying good health. They had been to the inyanger or doctor, who told them there was an Umturgatie (or witch) who occasioned their sickness, and that the doctor wanted a cow before he would point him out.' Isaacs went on to say: 'I could perceive their sickness had arisen from eating green corn, but told them I had no objection to give the cow, provided it would discover the object which caused such superstitious notions to affect them, or if it would recover the sick. They assured me it would, and I was induced to promise them a cow.'

Thus it was early observed that the belief in witchcraft involved the idea that Africans thought it 'singular that they alone should be sick while all the people around them were enjoying good health'. In this observation lay an important clue to understanding the system of beliefs in witchcraft and magic. Another clue was the observation, made by many administrators and missionaries, that men accused their personal enemies of bewitching them: wherefore, said these observers, the charges of witchcraft were obviously fraudulent. This alleged fraudulence is exhibited in the standard picture of the witch-doctor, the old woman Gagool in Rider Haggard's novel, *King Solomon's Mines*.

Indeed, it wasn't until a hundred years after Isaacs's diary was published that these separate clues were brought together by Professor Evans-Pritchard to explain the *logic*, the intellectual coherence, of witch-craft beliefs in their relation to natural events and to society. He did this in his analysis of *Witchcraft, Magic and Oracles among the Azande of the Anglo-Egyptian Sudan*. Subsequent research in other African tribes has con-firmed this analysis entirely.

Clearly from Isaacs's words, the belief in witchcraft explains not how a misfortune occurred, but why a particular person suffered that misfortune. It is said to be due to the powers of witchcraft possessed by someone who wished him harm—that is, a personal enemy. Bad feeling sets the power of witchcraft to work. But bad feeling does so in only certain kinds of relationship, and not in all relationships. Indeed, custom may exclude accusations of witchcraft from those relationships where difficulties and friction are greatest, as between a father and his son. For it is not believed that a father's feelings against a disobedient son set witchcraft to work. Evans-Pritchard laid the foundations for our understanding of the logic of witchcraft, and he pioneered our analysis of the more complex problem of why accusations of witchcraft arise in each tribe in some types of social relationship, and not in others.

I shall attempt to pursue these complex problems of who accuses whom of witchcraft in several tribes. Witchcraft fears and accusations breed quarrels between people: I want to explain how far they disrupt relationships between those people, and how far they lead to readjustments in social ties within a wider social order. This is the central theme of my lectures.

Young Nathaniel Isaacs noted that the Zulu 'seemed to think it singular that they alone should be sick while all the people around them were enjoying good health'—hence they thought a witch was at work. And if he had argued with them, as he noted in his diary, that their sickness was due to eating green corn, they would probably have replied: 'But these other people have also eaten green corn, and look, they are not sick'. Witchcraft as a theory of causation does not deny that men fall ill from eating certain foods, but it explains why some of them fall ill at some times and not at other times. What it is that belief in witchcraft explains emerges more clearly from what we call an accident. I knew a Zulu whose son was bitten by a snake and died. He said that his son had been killed by witchcraft. This did not mean that he didn't see that his son had been bitten by a snake, or that he didn't know that some snakes are poisonous while others are not, and that the bite of a poisonous snake may be fatal. When he said that his son was killed by witchcraft, he meant that a witch caused the snake to bite his son so that the son died.

For every misfortune, like every piece of good fortune, involves two questions: the first is 'how' did it occur, and the second is 'why' it occurred at all. The 'how' is answered by common-sense empirical observation: the son died because he was bitten by a poisonous snake. But this does not explain why that son was bitten by that snake and at that time and place, and not by another snake at another time and place; or indeed why that man was bitten and not some other man altogether. Beliefs in witchcraft explain why particular persons at particular times and places suffer particular misfortunes—accident, disease, and so forth. Witchcraft as a theory of causation is concerned with the singularity of misfortune.

Other cultures give different kinds of answers to this metaphysical problem, why certain events happen to certain people at certain times and places. There are the will of God or of gods, Kismet, Karma, Fate, Providence, the action of ancestral spirits. African tribes also employ some of these other answers to varying degrees. The agnostic scientist may call it 'chance', the intersection of two chains of events in space-time: a boy taking the cattle to water, trod on a snake sunning itself in the path.

Hence the belief in witchcraft does not of itself exclude a considerable amount of what we can rightly call empirical observation and reasoning about 'how' events occur. Indeed, the beliefs clearly involve this kind of reasoning. Because a witch cannot just harm people: he (or often she) harms them by using disease and crop-blight, by making elephants charge them or lions eat them or snakes bite them, by causing them when climbing a tree after a beehive to stand on branches which are rotten at their heart. No people could survive without an extensive technical knowledge. Their witchcraft beliefs operate inside this technical knowledge. To some extent, it is even possible for scientific understanding of the 'how' of a misfortune to increase, without disposing of the 'why' of the misfortune—that it was caused by witchcraft. A Pondo teacher in South Africa told Professor Monica Wilson: 'It may be quite true that typhus is carried by lice, but who sent the infected louse? Why did it bite one man and not another?'

Thus witchcraft as a theory of causation does not explain the whole of any misfortune. Every misfortune has its empirical side. And certain unfortunate events are clearly due to a man's own weaknesses. Thus if a man fails to exhibit proper technical skill in hunting, agriculture, or pot-making, he cannot expect his fellows to agree with him if he blames on witchcraft the startled game, a poor crop, or a pot cracked in firing. Similarly, if he lapses morally he cannot say that witchcraft made him sin. For witchcraft does not make a man lie, or steal, or commit adultery. A man must accept responsibility for his wrongdoings. Hence if a Zande murdered a fellow-tribesman with his spear he was tried in court by his chief and was convicted by evidence. He could not plead in defence that witchcraft made him commit murder. The situation was quite different when a man was killed by an enemy of a foreign tribe in battle. The enemy lived outside the control of the tribe, and he could not be arrested and tried. But by the Zande code the dead warrior's kin had to take vengeance for his death, and this was blamed on witchcraft within the tribe; witchcraft caused one man and not another man to be slain by a particular enemy in this battle. The witch was the internal murderer, from whom compensation could be demanded.

I have been describing how the belief in witchcraft as a theory of causation works, without mentioning the nature of the witch. For this is how the belief works in practice. Men suffer misfortunes and then believe that they have been attacked by a witch. In theory, of course, the witch has set his evil power to work and this has caused the misfortune. The Azande believe that witchcraft is a substance in the stomach whose soul goes out at night and harms others. Anyone may have this substance in his stomach, but not everyone sets it to work. If a man is upright—of sound principle, charitable, even-tempered, tolerant, generous—he will not set witchcraft to work even if he has it in his stomach. The Azande say it remains 'cool'. But if a man is quarrelsome, spiteful, bad-tempered, greedy, over-ambitious, his witchcraft will get 'hot' and go out at night to harm those against whom he bears grudges. Thus witchcraft as a theory of causation embraces a theory of morals, for it says that witches are wicked people. It is their wicked feelings which cause their witchcraft to do harm. Azande say: 'Jealousy comes first and witchcraft follows after'. The ethics of witchcraft thus disapprove of the common anti-social vices and approve of the virtues of many societies.

That the use of witchcraft is immoral is shown in the whole set of beliefs. Generally, African doctrine is not always altogether clear how far a witch is aware of what he is doing: ideas here vary from tribe to tribe. Mostly, the answer is that a person does not know what he is about when he begins killing; but after several crimes he realizes what is happening. But the doctrine is clear that unless a man has vicious feelings his witchcraft powers will do no harm. It is the use of witchcraft, and not its mere possession, which is immoral. The ethical wrongdoing involved is clearly exhibited by the sorcerers whom Evans-Pritchard contrasts with witches. A sorcerer is a man who has not witchcraft in his stomach, so that to harm others he has deliberately to take the wicked decision to use magical substances, rites, and spells against a fellow. Thus Zulu say that if you put a certain substance in a porcupine quill and stab an enemy's footprints you will afflict him with illness. It is important that among the Zulu, as in many other tribes, it is believed that men make this deliberate choice to do evil in these ways, while women are believed to be witches, who are possessed of innate evil power.

Any misfortune may be ascribed to this ill will of a witch, but if the trouble is slight Azande merely dismiss it as 'witchcraft', much as we might say 'bad luck'. The actual witch who is responsible is sought only if he has to be induced to remove a disease he is causing, or if he has caused a death—or rather, he used to be sought after a death, because this kind of witch-hunt has been banned by European governments. Few methods of seeking witches involve direct naming of the guilty person. More usually the sufferer puts the names of his personal enemies to the diviner or apparatus, in order to select from among them that enemy who has the power of witchcraft and who has used this power to cause the misfortune under investigation. The most important Zande technique consists in giving a substance, prepared with

G

special taboos, to chickens while asking questions. Each question is framed to allow of a 'yes' or 'no' answer to the problem, thus: 'if X is the witch who is making my son ill, poison-oracle, kill the chicken; if X is not the witch, poison-oracle, spare the chicken'. The substance is a strychnine poison so that the chicken will either be killed or will vomit it; and its operation cannot be controlled by the amount which is given to the chicken. Eventually the oracle is likely to say 'yes' to some enemy's name. Other techniques of divination work similarly.

It is clearly absurd to say that the detection of personal enemies as witches is fraudulent, because obviously it is reasonable that the witch who harms a man should be at odds with him. This is contained in the beliefs about witches themselves. The consultant in fact believes that all the persons whose names he submits to the oracle want to harm him: he wants to know which of them is working maleficently against him at the moment. In short, Evans-Pritchard clarified for us that the belief in witchcraft explains the 'why' of misfortune, and, through techniques of divination, he related this 'why' to personal animosities which cause men to wish others harm.

If the consultation is about an illness, the guilty witch has to be approached in certain customary ways to withdraw his witchcraft, and this he does with equal formality. If he reacts to the charge with anger, it is proof of his guilt and of his continued ill will. But if the witch is sought because he caused a death, the chief's oracle must confirm the verdict before he can be punished or required to pay compensation. In Central and South Africa he was required at the chief's orders to drink the oracle-poison himself. If he vomited it, he was declared innocent; if it stupefied him, he was guilty and might be killed. This ordeal had at least the merit that it was not death which proved innocence. When David Livingstone came across the ordeal on the Zambesi, he told his African followers about 'the water-test formerly in use in Scotland: the supposed witch, being bound hand and foot, was thrown into a pond; if she floated, she was considered guilty, taken out and burned; but if she sank and was drowned, she was pronounced innocent'. Livingstone, with his usual dry humour, added: 'The wisdom of my ancestors excited as much wonder in their minds as their custom did in mine'.

It is reasonable that the man who harms you should be your enemy. Or at least that you should feel that he is your enemy. For clearly the selection of a witch is guided by a man's own view of his personal relations, by his own grudges, ambitions, and similar sentiments. But his accusations also have to appear reasonable before a general public, which may well debate the situation in advance. For Africans themselves appreciate what is implied in the processes by which witchcraft accusations are made. A Barotse king declared that they were 'lies fostered by hate and envy'. I heard one of his councillors reprimand villagers who had accused an aged female relative of killing them. He said: 'You are ungrateful. She cared for you when she was young; now she is old and you have to look after her, you hate her. Let me hear no more of this.' Again, in Zululand I lived with an important and wealthy governor of a district. Cheek by jowl with his homestead was the homestead of a cousin, descended from the same grandfather. One of the cousin's wives died after a long and painful illness. After brooding on it for a while, the widower burst out with an accusation that the governor, who (he said) had always hated him, had killed her by sorcery. The whole district was upset by the quarrel. I discussed the case with an old diviner, who himself hunted sorcerers and witches. Yet fully aware of what the psychologists call projection, he concluded: 'Obviously the accusation is absurd. Why should the governor hate his cousin? The governor possesses political power and has inherited the main family herd. The cousin thinks the governor hates him, because he hates the governor.' So that Africans know that often a man accuses not someone who hates him, or who is envious of him, but someone whom he hates or envies. They may stress this when they themselves are accused, or if for any reason they side with another alleged witch; but they forget it when they make an accusation. In this partiality they are not unique among mankind.

I have been describing a fraction of the logic of beliefs in witchcraft, because unless we understand this much we cannot go on to the problems which are more interesting for a sociologist, the analysis of particular accusations in different tribes. This has been the field which has been developed by Evans-Pritchard's successors. Indeed, in the light of their later research, I find it difficult to see exactly how the Azande witchcraft charges work. For it is clear that a man does not make accusations indiscriminately against all those with whom he has difficulties and quarrels. Azande commoners dare not accuse the nobles who rule over them. And nobles do not accuse

one another of witchcraft, though they may impute
sorcery, for Azande believe that witchcraft descends
from father to son. As all nobles are related by descent
through males, if a noble accused another noble of
witchcraft, he would be accusing himself and all his
clan of having witchcraft in their stomachs, or alleging
that his fellow was a bastard. Again, therefore, a
commoner would not accuse his father, or his other
paternal kinsmen. Indeed, it seems to me striking
that in Azandeland witchcraft descends from father
to son, whereas among the patriarchal peoples of
South Africa it is transmitted from women to their
children—like haemophylia, it can be carried by men
but not passed on.

This whole situation suggests that the Azande beliefs
are so constructed as to exclude any accusation of
witchcraft from within the group of men who are
related to one another by descent through males. Yet
friction may be greatest inside this group. And this
group cannot have witchcraft inside its ranks because
it is the group which combines to demand compensation or vengeance against some outside witch who has
killed their kinsman. Therefore witchcraft is not just
hatred, it is hatred working in some social relationships
and not in others. We shall not be able to understand
the sociology of Azande witchcraft, as against its
intellectual logic, until we understand the significance
of the vengeance group in Azande society. It must
have great significance, for since the Anglo-Egyptian
Government prohibited accusations and demands for
compensation, the group has continued to demand
vengeance. It obtains vengeance now by making magic

to kill the witch responsible for the death of its kinsman, and, as people in the neighbourhood die, asking
the oracle which one was the witch. This is a development of old forms of punitive magic which were
legitimately used against unknown adulterers and
thieves: known thieves and adulterers could be prosecuted in court. The Azande accuse neighbours related
otherwise than by agnatic descent; their dealings with
those so related are handled by other beliefs. A father's
anger is mystically dangerous, but it does not lead to
witchcraft.

Anthropologists working in Southern and Central
Africa have explored more fully the problem of why
persons related in some ways to the sufferer are accused,
while persons related to him in other ways are not
accused. For example, whatever difficulties a Zulu
woman may have with her own son, the Zulu would
think him crazy if he accused her of bewitching him.
Mothers do not bewitch their own children among the
Zulu. But they may among the tribes of the Lake
Nyasa region. And Zulu measure the moral disintegration of their society in modern times by the fact that
men nowadays accuse their fathers of witchcraft,
which would have been unthinkable in the past. Yet
some Zulu sons have always harboured resentment
against their fathers' authority.

To answer these problems, we have to look at
accusations of witchcraft in several different ways. First,
the belief in witchcraft as the cause of some misfortunes
is part of the African answer to the general problem
of why misfortune and evil exist in the world. The
belief states that if men feel immoral sentiments
against others they may cause harm to these others.

Natural events and the morality of social relations are, so to speak, involved in one another. For the argument is that bad feeling between some sorts of people affects wild animals, the growth of crops, human health, and so forth. Society and its members and its natural environment form a single system of relations which are morally interdependent. Nothing happens by chance. Good fortune is due to harmony in particular social relationships; and disharmony in those social relationships leads to misfortune. A Yao hated his relative when he should have loved him. The relative went travelling and was sleeping against a wall with two men lying beside him: a lion stepped over the outside two and took his victim from against the wall. Hatred where it should not have existed led to death, for clearly witchcraft was at work. We do not, openly at least, believe in this involvement of social relations with natural events. The contrast between our views and those of Africans emerges graphically if we consider legal responsibility. In our society, you can sue a man for injury only if he has harmed you in some overt and observable manner; in a society which believes in witchcraft, every misfortune potentially founds a case against another for harming you.

Witchcraft beliefs are not unique in affirming this close relationship between the moral interaction of people, and what happens in the way of good and ill fortune. Ancestral cults embody similar ideas; but here the ancestral spirits punish people for not making due offerings to the spirits themselves, or for not observing their obligations to their kinsfolk. Witchcraft attacks the virtuous, ancestors attack the wicked. To be prosperous men must make sacrifices to their spirits, and they can only do this when they are in friendship with other members of the congregation. Otherwise the offering is spoilt. Sacrifices are the appropriate occasions for venting grievances: men must cleanse their hearts. An Anglican anthem similarly demands: 'See that ye love one another fervently'. But beliefs in the malice of witchcraft and in the wrath of ancestral spirits do more than ask this as an act of grace; they affirm that if you do not love one another fervently misfortune will come. Bad feeling is charged with mystical danger: virtue in itself produces order throughout the universe. Though a charge of witchcraft for causing a misfortune may exaggerate and exacerbate a quarrel, the belief emphasizes the threat to the wider social order which is contained in immoral sentiments. Hence the beliefs exert some pressure on men and women to observe the social virtues, and to feel the right sentiments, lest they be suspected of being witches. The beliefs act as a sanction against anti-social behaviour by supporting the social virtues. Thus the beliefs support the moral order of the community, over and above particular quarrels. Anger and hate are not only bad and sinful, as among ourselves, but they carry in them the mystical threat of disaster to others or to oneself. In religious beliefs virtues and values are clearly lifted out of the workaday world and placed on a spiritual plane where they are beyond question. Witchcraft beliefs by contrast invest wicked feelings with threats which they themselves do not contain, but which are charged with additional power.

This view of the universe is a small-scale view, appropriate to a small-scale society. It implies that wrongful conflicts between people destroy the single moral cohesion which embraces the community and its environment, by producing physically harmful results. Throughout these lectures I have been emphasizing two general characteristics of indigenous African society. It is organized in groupings of kin or small states where face-to-face relations are of paramount importance. There are few specialized relationships and these are not linked together in large-scale institutional arrangements. A man on the whole does everything with the same lot of other men—with them he earns his living, marries, and raises and educates his children, forms a political association, seeks his recreation, and worships his gods. As these close personal relationships serve most of men's interests, all events tend to be explained by what occurs in those relationships. If things go wrong, then your personal relations are bad: someone is harbouring a grievance against you. If someone harbours a grievance, then you are in danger. An immoral witch will attack you. Or if you do wrong, ancestral spirits will punish you.

The building up of community out of intensively interrelated groups of kinsfolk, with but few specialized relationships, is based on the stationary subsistence economies which are characteristic of Africa. All men, including even chiefs, live at approximately the same standard. They gain their living by simple tools and are heavily threatened by natural disasters. There is pressure on all men, and especially on the rich, to be generous in sharing: production is individualistic, but consumption is largely communal. What each man has to do is demarcated by his social position, and any failure to reach the standard is severely reprobated.

But so is any unusual success beyond a man's appropriate due. Exceptional achievement is bought at the cost of one's fellows. The man who is too successful is suspected of being a witch and himself is suspicious of the witchcraft of his envious fellows. Among the Bemba of Northern Rhodesia to find one beehive in the woods is luck, to find two is very good luck, to find three is witchcraft. Once in Barotseland during the dry season I joined a fishing-party at which a crowd of men entered a shallow pool and hurled spears blindly into the mud to get fish. Too few fishermen had arrived and the fish escaped to the empty parts of the pool. The catch was very small, and a councillor said to me, only half-jokingly: 'He who got fish to-day is a witch!' Was he digging at me? I had got four fish. I have known a man who built a fine house give up living in it because he believed that he had become the target of envious witches. This was one of many similar incidents, and all anthropologists report them.

African economic and political systems are limited so that ambitious men cannot create new enterprises nor seek for prestige in several different spheres. As a man grows up he comes into competition with his fellows for political position, and above all into competition with his own kinsmen for position and property. Hence it is not surprising to find that headmen of villages and men who gained political power are believed by many to do so by witchcraft. When a Yao headman in Nyasaland is installed his taste for human meat is tested in the installation ceremony: because Yao witches eat the corpses of those they kill.

I am trying to emphasize a general situation which

contrasts strongly with the kind of society which we know, the Britain which developed after the industrial revolution—which itself saw the official end to witch-craft charges. Since then we have lived in our families and had relations of a sentimental kind with our kin and friends, but we have not been dependent on them for most of our needs. Economic, religious, educational, political, recreational activities, all these associate with us persons who are not our relatives and with whom we may have little other contact. We are affected throughout each day by the operation of large-scale institutional organization, and not by the same few relatives and neighbours. We can move away from unpleasant situations in our natal families or at work, to establish ourselves elsewhere. If we, neverthe-less, blame disturbances in the working of these com-plicated institutional arrangements on the moral defects of particular people, it is not surprising that Africans, living so intensively in their small groups, see that moral relations in these groups are closely involved in all happenings.

A sociological understanding of charges of witch-craft has first to be sought in this general situation. There are straightforward occasions of competition to which particular misfortunes can be ascribed. A very common one throughout Africa is the charge that may be made between two wives of one man, for they are competing for his sexual and other favours, and for the interests of their children. Men with equal claims to the headmanship of a village strive against one another, and the victor is suspected of triumphing through witchcraft. But the working out of other charges, and of certain specific forms of beliefs in different tribes, involves deeper analysis of the personal difficulties and struggles which at a particular moment may lie behind accusing someone of witchcraft. Increasingly we are finding that the charge of witchcraft may in effect be produced by the working out through time of two contradictory social processes within the group. These focus on a particular person, and the charge of witchcraft enables the rupture of the disturbed relationship to be effected with social approval.

Among the Zulu, domestic and kinship life centres on the linking together of men related to one another through males. There are strong animosities among these men, arising from living together itself, and from competition for the property and the positions of the group. Yet charges of witchcraft are still not often made by these men against one another. Much more frequently, they blame their misfortunes upon the women who have married into the group, on daughters-in-law and on sisters-in-law. Or their mothers bring charges against their wives. These are the strangers in the group who can be held responsible, through their ill-nature, for the ills of the group without destroying the loyalty of the group. But as outsiders we can say that these wives are socially responsible for many of the conflicts between the closely related men; for it is through their wives, and the children to whom these wives give birth, that men want to become independent of their fathers and brothers. This is as true of Zululand as it is of England; and in Hindu India wives were blamed for the break-up of large joint families of related men. A wife gives a man sons who strengthen his group and build up its power; but they are also independent persons who will force their father into competition with his brothers, and in turn will compete among themselves. Hence the growth in numbers of the group through the women who bear its children both strengthens the group and introduces dissension into it; and the wives are the focus of two conflicting social processes. They are seen as centres of mystical evil arising from their very ill-nature, which attracts to itself sexual familiars who begin to demand the lives of their relatives. If Zulu men wish to harm others, they have deliberately to enter on the arts of sorcery.

This Zulu example shows that even when we are dealing with the apparently straightforward sexual competition between the two wives of one man, we may have to seek below the surface. Here, too, conflicts arise between the pulls of different social allegiances, which are not ultimately reconcilable. The two wives have two sets of children who compete for limited power and property, and who cannot set out on their own to build up a livelihood. Children are desired by a Zulu kinship-group because they strengthen it: in the end this increase in numbers leads to the group's breaking up. The Zulu appear partly to conceal this fundamental conflict from themselves by the argument that it is not competition between men which leads to rupture of relations, but wickedness on the part of the wives—who, in sociological fact, have bred the conflict, by producing the destructive children who are so desired. To protect their wives from these charges the men leave the group, but not of their own free will—apparently. The values of enduring loyalty to their fellow agnates, and of their own determination to live together, are not disobeyed. They go away because of their stranger-wives. And once they are in separate villages the situations producing the witchcraft charges become fewer in number and less acute: the different villages re-establish relations of a similar kind but at greater distance.

Fundamentally, the same situation, in essence, has been reported from the matrilineal tribes of Nyasaland, where position and property pass from mother's brother to sister's son. The social power of a man depends on his control of his sisters and their children. When a young man grows up he tries to take his sisters away from the control of their mother's brother. His legitimate desire for independence and his customary rights to guardianship over his sisters and their children conflict with the equally legitimate customary rights of the senior man. Sickness among his sisters or their offspring, ascribed to the uncle's witchcraft, allows the younger man to assert his rights, and take his sisters away. The mystical exaggeration of the power in wicked feelings allows rupture of relations and breach of the value of village and kinship-group unity. Again, the new village sets up more distant, but friendly, relations with the old village.

Witchcraft beliefs are the source of many disharmonies and quarrels: no anthropologist would deny this. But accusations of witchcraft also sometimes solve quarrels which arise between men from the conflict between allegiances to different and contradictory social principles. Thus the accusations allow new relationships to be set up, and new types of friendship to be established. In some respects, at least, the operation of the beliefs validates my general thesis. Custom creates conflicts, in certain ranges of social relations;

it also resolves them when the wider social order is examined. If people had no wickedness in them, theoretically all social alterations could be carried out peaceably, or no alterations would be necessary.

African life nowadays is changing rapidly, and witchcraft accusations now involve circumstances arising from Africa's absorption in Western economy and polity. Conflicts between old and new social principles produce new animosities, which are not controlled by custom, and these open the way to new forms of accusation. Charges, previously excluded, as by a Zulu against his father, are now made. The system of witchcraft beliefs, originally tied to certain social relations, can be adapted to new situations of conflict— to competition for jobs in towns, to the rising standard of living, made possible by new goods, which breaches the previous egalitarianism, and so forth. In response to this situation there have arisen in Africa movements designed to cleanse the country of witches, held responsible for social disintegration, for falling yields on over-cultivated lands, for new diseases. The philosophy of these movements against witchcraft is that if Africans would cease to hate one another and would love each other, misfortune would pass. These movements are short-lived, and they tend to be replaced by religious movements involving messianic elements.

We see that indigenous witchcraft beliefs are incompatible with our highly productive economy, and its emphasis on individual achievement and on raising one's own standard of living. They also seem to me to be incompatible with the emergence of the family of parents and children as the important group at the expense of the former extended kinship groupings.

This process accompanies industrialization. The members of the family cease to be linked for important purposes with other kin, but become involved with unrelated persons in the specialized relationships within a large-scale impersonal set of institutions. During the years when the industrial system is becoming established in Africa, the increase of conflicts in personal relationships and in the organizing principles of social life has led to an increase in fears and charges of witchcraft, as happened at the beginning of our own industrial revolution. Nor are these fears and charges controlled by old sanctions.

The difficulty of destroying beliefs in witchcraft is that they form a system which can absorb and explain many failures and apparently contradictory evidence. Evans-Pritchard shows that the theory involved is a complete whole, in which every part buttresses every other part. Illness proves that a witch is at work, he is discovered by divination, he is persuaded to withdraw his witchcraft—the patient recovers, as most patients do recover. Or counter-magic used against the witch appears to be successful.

Nor are men required to look at the system as a whole at any one moment. They see it situationally. When you accuse your enemy of bewitching you, the system seems reasonable; when he accuses you, and you consider you are innocent, you can use other beliefs to explain away the charge as ridiculous. You can say he did not really consult an oracle, or that the true witch influenced the operation of the oracle, or that a taboo in the working of the oracle was broken and it just killed chickens.

This sort of system of belief is characterized by what

Evans-Pritchard has called 'secondary elaboration of belief'. In most cases magic does not attempt the impossible: rain-magicians do not make rain in the dry season, and magic against thieves is made against unknown persons, not named persons. Hence there will be many successes, which are remembered. The failures can be interpreted within the system by invoking other beliefs. Every year before the Trade Winds bring their rains, Zulu call in special magicians to treat their villages against lightning. Most villages are not struck, but if a man's village *is* struck, he will say the magician was bad, his medicines were poor, a taboo was broken, a witch wielded the lightning, or Heaven itself was powerfully determined to strike the village. We reason similarly. If your house, which you have protected with lightning conductors, is nevertheless struck, you may say that the workman was bad, the wires poor, a rule of craft in installation was broken, the charge was too strong. You do not rush to the Royal Society to deny the validity of scientific theory. The total system of beliefs thus allows for a good deal of failure. It also allows for the existence of scepticism. But generally it is scepticism about particular charges of witchcraft, particular lots of oracle-poison, particular magical substances, and particular magicians or witch-doctors. Evans-Pritchard gives one example which drives this point hard home. In Africa witches are believed to cause illness by shooting objects into their victim; the doctor should extract these objects to effect a cure. Of course, doctors produce these objects by sleight of hand in poultices or by concealing them in their mouths. But not even the doctor doubts the belief as such. He regrets only

H

that he does not possess the magic—which the doctor in the next district may have—to enable him really to extract the noxious object. Meantime, he has to pretend to do this extraction for that peace of mind of the patient which is necessary for recovery.

As scepticism develops it may take curious forms. I once heard two of my African clerks arguing about beliefs in sorcery. One asserted that you could attack a man by stabbing his footprints with a porcupine quill containing noxious substances. The other retorted: 'What, even if he is wearing shoes?'

This part of Evans-Pritchard's analysis illuminates the circular nature of reasoning in all systems of social thought. Practically all societies have stereotyped ideas about different categories of people. Experience is carefully sifted, by selection of incidents which support the stereotypes, to maintain the system as a whole. And if experience contradicts the system, there is always the individual exception. When Christians use the phrase 'he is a decent Jew' they confirm their stereotype that most Jews are not decent, since they know only a few Jews. And Jews may reason similarly about Christians, Whites about Blacks, and Blacks about Whites, employers and employees about one another.

To break into the closed circle is immensely difficult. I remember finding on a friend's bookshelf before the war a collection of anti-Hitler cartoons from all over the world. I turned to the title-page and saw the imprint 'Leipzig: collected by Ernst Hanfstaengel', who was personal aide-de-camp to Hitler. Those cartoons, which portrayed Hitler as a fool, a beast, a mountebank, and so on, were re-published in Germany by the Nazis to prove to Germans that Germany was encircled, and that other lands were ruled by Communistic Capitalistic Jews who encouraged these vilifications of the Führer. The moral for propaganda is clear: direct assault on a closed system of ideas is not easy, since the system absorbs the attacks and converts them to strengthen itself. That lice carry typhus is easily absorbed into the belief in witchcraft. Only developed science has outside criteria of truth and falsehood.

Usually, people whose beliefs are attacked remind me of the man who thought he was dead. After long argument, the psychiatrist asked him: 'Tell me, do dead men bleed?' 'Of course not, every fool knows that dead men don't bleed', came the reply. The doctor then seized a scalpel and triumphantly cut the patient's hand: 'There you are, you're not dead'. But the patient held up his bleeding hand: 'Golly . . . golly . . . Dead men *do* bleed'. Is this so different from the trade union secretary who denied that trade union leaders had lost touch with the rank and file, but asserted that the rank and file had lost touch with their leaders?

Evans-Pritchard's study thus not only explained Azande witchcraft itself to us, but he also showed that Azande, reasoning within the premisses of their system, think much as we do with our social and even scientific beliefs. I don't mean that the psychic and mental life of a person who believes in witchcraft is precisely the same as the psychic life of a man who does not. But it is clear that conscious ratiocination within the system of magic and witchcraft is sufficiently similar to our own modes of reasoning for us to understand and recognize its processes. Perhaps, aside from a few sceptics, only the scientist in his laboratory regularly checks his premises and assumptions so as to escape being bound in the same way; though Professor Polanyi has used Evans-Pritchard's analysis to illuminate even the nature of scientific thought. But above all this analysis, by the very exoticism of the beliefs involved, focuses attention on certain problems in our own systems of thinking about social relationships.

The belief in witchcraft, as the cause of why misfortunes occur, was officially banned in England in the reign of James II. But in other forms the same kind of belief still seems to persist. An essential feature of African beliefs in witchcraft is that they predicate in advance that someone within a certain category of persons is responsible for natural misfortunes, when he cannot be—we know—in fact so responsible. On the whole, we no longer search for persons on whom we can blame *natural* misfortunes. Though I think we can say that the Nazis tended to do this with Jews. But we are not so ready to accept that *social* disturbances are an inevitable part of the life of man on earth, and there are many systems of belief throughout the modern world which ascribe quarrels in society to the vicious character of certain categories of persons.

Appropriately enough, we call searches for these persons 'witch-hunts'. I do not, of course, suggest that persons opposed to a particular social arrangement never intrigue and damage: obviously they do. But all too frequently in our history men have shown that they will blame and punish a certain category of persons for ills which are due to physical causes or the working of society itself. Certainly these condemned categories are liable to be blamed for some social disturbances, or the extent of disturbances, beyond their due. Some of us can see this clearly in the cruder forms of the witch-hunt. But other witch-hunts are less obvious. Anyone with some knowledge of the uncertainties involved in loading and unloading ships in England's tidal ports would expect that the dockers would have a series of grievances likely to provoke dispute, and that the tempo of disputation would be accelerated by the constant necessity of bargaining over rates of pay. Yet when disputes arise they are blamed on agitators by those officials who represent the dockers.

The developed industrial organization of a modern nation is so complicated, and the process of maintaining it so complex, that again one would expect there to be constant breakdowns in planning and communication, and that human frailty would lead to constant miscalculation. Yet it is difficult for men to accept this; and only too easy for them to blame failures on red-tape civil servants, inefficient executives, counter-revolutionaries, saboteurs, and the like. It is even more difficult to accept that a nation contains real conflicts of interest between local areas, classes, or other groups, and that these are not in fact eliminated by the ideals of ultimate amity and unity.

For it is difficult for us to accept that our own society also embodies contradictory principles and processes. These involve conflict. We allow room for divergence of opinion, and indeed interest, but within defined limits. If the limits are overstepped, the witch-hunt may begin. It is a witch-hunt so long as persons are blamed for misfortunes that they are not responsible for. The hunt may, as in Africa, temporarily resolve conflicts. But though I have argued that African beliefs resolve, as well as create, conflicts of allegiance, I have not suggested that it is the best way of doing this. Beliefs in magic and witchcraft help to distract attention from the real causes of natural misfortune. They also help to prevent men from seeing the real nature of conflicts between social allegiances. We can only hope that it may yet be possible to run a society without any of this kind of distracting obscurity.

V

THE LICENCE IN RITUAL

IN certain armed services at Christmas, and at Christmas only, the officers wait at table on the men. This kind of reversal of rôle is well-known in ceremonial and ritual. It was one of the problems which lay at the heart of Sir James Frazer's monumental study, *The Golden Bough*. In his attempt to interpret the situation of the Roman priest-king who had to defend his life against his would-be successor, Frazer went on to consider ceremonies in which people of lower social categories are made temporary kings, in which women act as men and men act as women, and so forth. These rites of reversal obviously include a protest against the established order. Yet they are intended to preserve and even to strengthen the established order; and in many rituals their performance is believed to achieve success and prosperity for the group which practises them. Therefore they fall squarely within the general problem which I am discussing in this series of lectures—the problem of how custom in Africa emphasizes conflicts in certain ranges of social relationship and yet establishes cohesion in the wider society or over a longer period of time. It is with this problem in mind that I am going to try to interpret ceremonies in which women don men's clothing and do things normally prohibited to them, such as herding cattle, and also to interpret great political feasts in which kings are pitied and insulted and threatened.

Before I go on with this description and its interpretation, I must stress that African ritual and religion form a vast field of study. Many psychological and sociological—indeed physiological—combinations are required for a full analysis. I am not attempting this impossible task. I am discussing only one aspect of ritual—how its protest against the established order is licensed and even encouraged. This encouragement must be explained by some theory which demonstrates that the ritual is socially valuable. And I am going to deal mainly with rituals which contain this element of protest—which are organized to exhibit rebellion. There are many rituals which are not organized thus.

I start from the empirical fact that African rituals are frequently organized to exhibit rebellion and protest, and to emphasize the conflicts which exist between those who participate in the rituals. Thus there are descriptions of Zulu agricultural rites—no longer performed— in which women and girls committed public obscenities and acted as if they were men. More strikingly, the ceremonies were said to be performed in order to propitiate a certain goddess named Nomkubulwana. She is described 'as being robed with light as a garment and having come down from heaven to teach people to make beer, to plant, to harvest, and all the useful arts. . . . She is a maiden and she makes her visit to the earth in the Spring of the year. She is also described as presenting the appearance of a beautiful landscape with verdant forests on some parts of her body, grass-covered slopes on others, and cultivated slopes on others. She is said to be the maker of the rain.' The ceremonies to supplicate a good harvest from the goddess were comparatively simple. I describe only their core. The young unmarried girls donned men's garments and carried shields and assagais. They drove the cattle out to pasture and milked them, though cattle were normally taboo to females. Meanwhile their mothers planned a garden for the goddess far out in the veld, and poured a libation of beer to her. Thereafter this garden was neglected. At various stages of the ceremonies women and girls went naked, and sang lewd songs. Men and boys hid inside the huts, and might not go near the women. If they did, the women and girls could attack them.

This goddess and her ceremonies are interesting for many reasons. The Zulu and other South African tribes have very little mythology and have not elaborated descriptions of any other of their spirits—of their High-God who, after making the world, withdrew from direct interest in it, or of the power of the Sky, or of ancestral spirits. Why should there be this clearer idea of an unusual naturalistic anthropomorphic goddess, connected with rites in which women behaved both lewdly and as if they were men? A search for the information on the surrounding tribes produced no similar goddess, but I found in them items of these lewd and other protests by women against established rules. To the south, the Tembu women behaved thus when they were celebrating a girl's puberty; to the north, Tsonga women went naked and sang lewd songs and maltreated any man they might meet, when they were trying to get rid of a crop-pest. These obscene and domineering acts by the women were encouraged, for they were believed to achieve a blessing for the community—good crops, the fertility and good health of a nubile girl, the riddance of crop-pest. I am recounting here the personal experience which first brought me up against the problem of how the customary exaggeration of conflict achieves a social blessing; and beyond that, the problem of how conflicts are built into a system of social order.

I set out to trace the rôles of women in all other social situations. I found that there were a whole series of beliefs and customs which emphasized that women as such were ritually ambivalent for the Zulu—that is, they had in them power for evil, and power for good. The power for evil existed in them independently of their conscious volition. Whenever they menstruated they threatened danger to warriors, crops, and cattle, by what we call supernatural means. They became witches harming others, by attracting to themselves sexual familiars. As ancestral-spirits, they were capriciously evil, while male spirits sent merited misfortune. These beliefs were extended into the wider world, for dangerous forked lightning was female, and sheet lightning was male. And so forth. On the other hand, their menstrual blood was important for it helped to make children, and their pregnant condition was magically fertilizing. The striking fact was that these capacities for good and for evil were inherent in being a female. Men had no such conflicting capacities, in their very nature as men. Men had deliberately to seek to do magical evil, by performing actions of sorcery. They could learn to be good magicians. But for women to become good magicians they had to undergo a painful illness ascribed to possession by a spirit. This was the ritual difference between men and women.

After surveying Zulu culture, I worked out that a woman was in law—in law, not always in practice—subject to the control of some man—either her father or brother, or after marriage her husband. The prime effect of this subordination was to give these men control over the woman's capacities as wife and as child-bearer. In exchange for transferring to the husband a woman's capacity as a wife, including her work in the gardens, and her capacity as a bearer of children, the husband handed over to her male relatives cattle which were taboo to her—she could not touch them or go into their corral. Here there seemed to me to be a fundamental conflict involved in the social position of a woman in Zulu society, a conflict which I've described in earlier lectures, but which I sharpen now in order to focus the problems of ritual. Zulu kinship groups are built on the principle of descent from men going on through men; succession to office and inheritance of property pass in this line, and the line of descent through women is completely excluded. That is, the line of descent through women as sisters and as daughters transmitted neither power nor property. But in practice the line of a man descends to his sons through his wife or wives. The Romans had a similar system, and they have a paradoxical legal maxim which sums up admirably this conflict which centres on the woman: *mulier et origo et finis familiae est*—a woman is the beginning and the end of a family. In Roman and Zulu society a woman as wife perpetuates her husband's line, as a daughter she is the end of her father's line. And her transference to the position of wife from that of daughter is achieved by the wedding-ceremony, in which she carries a man's shield and assagai, and by the handing-over of cattle.

Other evidence showed strongly that the approach of marriage was a period of great distress for Zulu girls: they were subject to frequent attacks of hysteria which were ascribed to the love-magic of their suitors. Marriage itself was a difficult relation, requiring adjustment to a strange family where the girl was hedged with many taboos. She had to avoid important parts of her husband's home village and even parts of her own hut. She had to alter her language so as not to use any word containing the root of her husband's name or the names of her senior male relatives-in-law. Her stressed function was to be a dutiful, hard-working, faithful, and decorous wife, bearing children for her husband, and caring for those children. Only when they grew up, could she become independent, as the mother of grown sons. And after her death it was believed that her spirit would send them capricious misfortune, not deserved by evil deeds; nor would she withdraw it after sacrifice, as a male spirit did. But in fulfilling her duty as a wife, she weakened her husband's group as well as strengthening it. On the one hand she gave her husband's group more members, fresh recruits; and on the other hand she produced competitors for power and for property in the group. Here is a second conflict in the position of a woman in these groups. These conflicts centring on the position of woman as wife and as child-bearer both hinge on the cattle which regulate Zulu marriage—Zulu say, therefore, 'cattle beget children'. Hence it seemed to me that cattle, and the herding of cattle, might well symbolize the whole legal subordination of women. Allowing them to herd the cattle would be a reward and a release, especially while they were also allowed to go naked and sing lewd songs and attack wandering men. This statement, that performing these normally tabooed actions is a reward and release, seems to be justified by the descriptions we have. But part of its interpretation involves psychological analysis for which there is no evidence.

Socially, the lifting of the normal taboos and restraints obviously serves to emphasize them. It is this aspect of the ceremony which most interests me. Zulu custom emphasizes the difference between men and women, beyond their biological differences. Women cannot approach cattle; women must be decorous in public; women do not take part in national life or national ceremonies; women, when they menstruate, are full of mystical danger. This is part of woman's social position, and the customs and beliefs emphasize her distinction and her separateness from men. For men herd cattle, they can be forward in national life and in national ceremonies, they do not menstruate and are not full of this mystical danger. But on one occasion in the year—the time of planting when they begin their arduous agricultural labours—women are allowed to act as if they were men. They are not only licensed to do so, but they are encouraged and even enjoined to do so in the interests of the community. When I was working in Zululand in 1937 these ceremonies were no longer performed: old men told me that therefore crops were poor. Hence the lifting of the taboos not only rewarded the women but it also brought benefits to the men who allowed this lifting and subjected themselves to the temporarily dominant women. I suggest that this was possible, and effective in ways we do not yet fully understand, because the women as well as the men accepted the general nature of Zulu society as good and valuable. That is, this particular ritual, by allowing people to behave in normally prohibited ways, gave expression, in a reversed form, to the normal rightness of a particular kind of social order. And the ritual would continue to be effective in this sense, and yet be rewarding to the women, so long as the women accepted Zulu arrangements as good. They were not suffragettes and feminists seeking to alter Zulu society in order to strengthen their own position. Had they been in revolt against Zulu rules, the ritual could not be effective in stating moral principles by reversal, with the belief that this reversal would bring the social blessing of rich harvests.

My analysis of the deeper social alignments affecting the position of women in this ritual is supported when we examine other rites among these peoples. Take this description of the Tsonga ritual which organizes the moving of a village. A Tsonga village is inhabited by a headman, with his wives and children, and the wives and children of his married sons. When they are ready to move, the headman goes first to examine some spots where he would like to build. He breaks small twigs from various trees and these are tested by the divining bones to see which spot will be prosperous. Building material is then collected at the chosen spot, and the headman and his principal wife leave the old village finally. They have ritual sexual relations on the new site and in the morning tie a knot in grass over which all the villagers should step. This ties the village to the headman and his principal wife. Now begins a month of taboo, especially on sexual relations by the villagers. Breach of this taboo may make the headman ill; it does not make the offender ill. The huts of the old village are carried to the new site by the men, who sing obscene songs insulting the women. Later when the women smear the floors of the huts with mud they retaliate with obscene songs at the men's expense. A Tsonga said of these songs: 'The village is broken to pieces, so are the ordinary laws. The insults which are taboo are now allowed.' The village is fenced with magical substances to obstruct the entry of witches. Finally the new home is ready. All couples have ritual sexual relations in order of precedence, and then the final rite of establishing the headman has to be performed. The headman's principal wife takes his assagai and shield and closes the gate of the village. She makes an offering to the ancestral spirits and prays for the people: 'Be not tied by the village! Bring forth children; live and be happy and get everything. You gods, see! I have no bitterness in my heart. It is pure. I was angry because my husband abandoned me, he said I was not his wife; he loved his younger wives. Now, this is finished in my heart. We shall have friendly relations together.' They then feast together.

This ceremony again requires that in the ritual there should be an emphatic statement of those conflicts within the village which are likely to lead to its breakup. In the end, indeed, over time these conflicts do lead to the splitting of the village. The conflicts centre on the marital relations of the different men in the village;

for through these marital relations each man gets children who may eventually enable him to set up his own village. Sexual relations are therefore banned during the period when the old village is deserted but the new village is not yet built—the period when dissident villagers may decide to leave. Normal restraints are lifted and obscenity is allowed. And a breach of the taboo on marital relations does not lead to mystical punishment of the wrongdoer, but to mystical threats to the headman. For it is his authority which is threatened by the marriages which lead to the independence of each man from the group. Finally, the principal wife takes the place of her husband, carrying his weapons, to symbolize the unity of the group of males and their wives, despite the fact that it is through the wives, who bear children, that the group will ultimately split. Women and men are shown to be identified in the interests of village unity. In her prayer the principal wife states the conflicts which exist between herself and other wives of the headman. She says they are jealous for his attentions; but it is also because they are jealous for the rights of their own children. The general opposition of the group of male kin to the stranger women whom they marry, and who bring dissension into the village, is stated in the obscene songs. This ritual again emphasizes conflicts which threaten the unity of the village. And it is carried out even if in practice everyone lives together harmoniously. But by this statement of the conflicts, the ritual emphasizes that the conflicts exist, and indeed it may exaggerate them. Yet the Tsonga believe that the effect of the ceremony is to bless the village with fertility and prosperity. This belief can be held so long as the members of the village accept the unity of the village as a good thing.

These same conflicts appear in many other rituals of these tribes. The desire of each group of male kin for wives, and yet their rejection of the wives as trouble-makers between them, is clearly stated in Zulu wedding ceremonies. The two intermarrying groups insult one another and threaten one another with weapons, they dance competitively against one another, the bride attempts to run away and has to be captured by her husband. Most clearly, this symbolism appears in the bride's carrying a small shield and a knife or assagai, as if she were a man, an enemy threatening her husband's group. And for long periods of the ceremony she has to sit with downcast head while her husband's kin insult her as a lazy good-for-nothing, of bad family, who is going to introduce quarrels into their happy home. Again, the ritual of marriage states in advance the conflicts that will hinge on her position, and this statement is believed to bless the marriage. Open expression of conflict within the group is believed to bring success, and to achieve the unity and prosperity of the wider group.

These rituals contain the belief that if people perform certain actions they will influence the course of events so that their group be made richer, more prosperous, more successful, and so forth. Some of us therefore call these actions 'ritual', and say that they contain 'mystical notions'—notions that their performance will in some mysterious way affect the course of events. 'Ritual' in this definition is contrasted with 'ceremonial' which consists of similar actions but has no such mystical notions associated with it.

I

Rituals of this kind, in which people perform actions in terms of their social rôles, are very widespread in the so-called primitive societies. They occur in the round of agriculture, in hunting and herding and manufacturing, and in military operations. They also occur when villages are moved or established and persons of authority are installed, and at different stages during the growing-up of individuals—at birth, puberty, marriage. Finally, they are important in funerals. We find that different societies ritualize these events to very different degrees, and different societies seize on different occasions to perform ritual. But overall a high ritualization of these social occasions is characteristic of the simpler societies, when compared with developed industrial civilizations. This rule is general, not absolute: for many simple societies, including those which belong to Islam, are not thus full of ritual.

The characteristic feature of this type of ritualization is that it makes use of the details of particular social relationships—of relationships between parents and children, maternal uncle and sister's son, men and women, king and princes and subjects. Indeed, the performance of specific ritual acts by persons in a particular kind of relationship with one another, is an essential element of that relationship. In many patriarchal societies, for example, it is the mother's brother who offers support to a lad at certain crises, by assisting him through initiation and other rituals. And provision of this ritual support, or the perform-ance of any rite in a ceremony involving some related person, is strongly enforced. Failure to conform is believed to lead to severe mystical penalties. Thus these ritual obligations are a very significant part of each relationship, and mark it off from other relationships. The varying ritual rôle of any person marks out his or her particular relationship with the person concerned; and the mystical penalties ensure that attention shall be paid to this rôle.

This being so, the ritual of each African tribe is built about the framework of its own forms of organization. Generally each tribe has distinctive sets of rituals for particular occasions, and in these rituals persons appear according to their relationships with one another in secular life. What happens is, that the various persons involved act out their rôles, either directly or by reversal of normal behaviour or by special symbolic rites. The Zulu bride carries shield and assagai, but she also carries a child of her husband's village on her back. She aggressively hurls an assagai into her husband's cattle-kraal; but she also meekly and ceremoniously collects firewood, cooks, and sweeps. In one set of rites she reverses her rôle, in the other set of rites she performs her future duties. The rites thus exhibit the ambivalence of her total rôle. In national ceremonies the king is insulted; but he is also lauded as all-powerful.

To say that African rituals have this high degree of particularism is not to deny that they deal with some of the general problems of social and human existence which have faced men everywhere. Some problems are universal. What is man? Whence does he come and whither does he go? Why should there be good and evil, prosperity and misfortune? How is human society set in the world of nature? What of the relations of men and women, parents and children, magistrates and people? What of the dealings of different groups with one another? These problems may be summed up, perhaps, in the general question: What is man's place, as a member of society, in the world? The answer is given partly in myth and legend, partly in dogma, and largely in rituals, like the Zulu ritual of women propitiating the goddess Nomkubulwana.

Africans have not worked out elaborate dogmas to explain the nature of the universe, though there are important exceptions to this generalization. Partly, they lack professional theologians. Hence, too, they do not strive to make their dogmas consistent. Their different rituals often embody inconsistent, and even contradictory, principles and values. For they reflect the existence in social life of different principles of social organization, which work out against each other, as we have seen. A wife is a blessing and a danger. These different principles compensate for one another, so that after a period of time or in a wider range of social relations conflicts in particular relationships are redressed, and the social pattern is re-established or duplicated. The village remains united, or two similar villages are built. This repetitive process in African social life allows the use of ritual statement of conflict. For social processes are working through quarrels and disputes to produce the same kind of social relationships, and not different new relationships. After their orgy of cattle-herding, Zulu women return to their daily tasks: they do not seek for a different set of feminist laws. The rituals are statements of rebellion, and never of revolution.

This tendency appears very markedly in the great national ceremonies of the tribes who dwell in South-east Africa. At sowing, first fruits and harvest, and before war, the Zulu nation performed, and the Swazi still perform, great military rituals. These rituals are believed to strengthen the nation, and to ensure national prosperity and victory. Yet they consist largely of statements of rebellion against the king, by his brother-princes and by his subjects, and of affirmations that he is unworthy of his high office. Dr. Hilda Kuper has brought this out in a brilliant description and analysis of the Swazi ceremonies. She also brings out the smallness of the universe within which Swazi cosmology is established, and the particularistic nature of their answer to the problem, what is man? The world is seen as a setting for the Swazi, in competition with neighbouring nations, and not for humanity in general. The king has to race the sun by beginning the first fruits ceremony before the sun reaches the Tropic of Capricorn; but he has also to begin the ceremony at the last wane of the moon when man's powers go into decline, in order that a fortnight later the ritual climax may occur at the full moon when man's powers are at their height.

The ceremony itself is strikingly an acting out of the whole of Swazi political relations, so that Dr. Kuper calls it 'a drama of kingship'. The king and queen-mother and queens, princes and councillors, men in their regiments, commoner chiefs, women, all have specific rôles in the ritual which are related to their rôles in everyday life. But the rites affirm not only the unity of the nation about the kingship, but also all the conflicts around the person of the reigning king: the resentment of his subjects against authority, the jealousy of his brother-princes who covet the throne, and so forth. Indeed, the ritual exaggerates the conflicts. Whether or not princes covet the throne they are made to act as if they do so covet it. At critical points when loyalty to the king is being affirmed, they have to leave the arena. And even their unborn children are also involved in the conflict—for the pregnant wife of a prince must also withdraw. At particular points in the ceremony a black bull is required: these bulls are stolen from commoner subjects who are thus made 'angry and proud', say the Swazi—an apt description of the ambivalent attitudes involved in being a member of an authoritative nation. There are, of course, also rites which affirm the support of the king both by princes and by subjects, but the general tone is as much one of rejection of the king as of triumph in his might. Here are typical songs:

> You hate the child king,
> You hate the child king;
>> *and*
> You hate him,
> Mother, the enemies are the people,
> You hate him,
> The people are wizards.
> Admit the treason of Mabedla—
> You hate him,
> You have wronged,
> Bend great neck,
> Those and those they hate him,
> They hate the king;
>> *and*
> King, alas for thy fate,
> King, they reject thee,
> King, they hate thee.

Those who hate the king are those who reject him: enemies within the tribe, not external enemies, his brothers and his discontented subjects. His fate is sad because he carries the burden of office, and the hatred that is the lot of office.

This theme of rejection and hatred of the king is so built into this great national ceremony that we have to ask, again, how the affirmation of rebellion can be so strong in a ritual which the people believe unifies and blesses their nation. And the king not only allows them to reject, and also to insult him; by doing so they are believed to support him in his arduous office.

Obviously there may be high psychological catharsis and relief in the princes and subjects who are required thus publicly to express hidden resentments. This problem lies outside my province. But again, as a sociologist, I am interested in the fact that this affirmation of rebellion goes on within an accepted order. The kingship is sacred, and its sacred strength is necessary for the nation—not only for its political strength, but also for the fertility of its women, fields, and cattle. The acceptance of the established order as right and good, and even sacred, seems to allow unbridled licence, very rituals of rebellion, for the order itself keeps this rebellion within bounds. Hence to act the conflicts, whether directly or by inversion or in other symbolical forms, emphasizes the social cohesion within which the conflicts exist. As the social order always contains a division of rights and duties, and of privileges and powers as against responsibilities, the ritual enactment of the order states its rightness. The ritual states that in virtue of their social position princes and people hate the king, but nevertheless they support him. They support him despite the conflicts between them. Or, at least, if they don't support the particular king, they support the kingship. For in the conditions of Swazi polity, as I've explained in an earlier lecture, malcontents did not attempt to subvert the social order, but to install a new king in the old kingship. Swazi were rebels, never revolutionaries. Should a particular king be a tyrant, his people's redress was not to seek to establish a republic, but to find some good prince in the king's family; for only a member of that family could hold the sacred kingship.

I myself believe that in the undeveloped Swazi economy, with its poor communications, different territorial sections of the nation developed strong autonomous tendencies, and tendencies to break out of the national hegemony. But these tendencies to fragment were canalized into a struggle to put particular princes on to the throne: the sections fought for the sacred kingship, and not for independence from it. Hence I have argued that in these African states periodic rebellions strengthened, and did not weaken, the political system. If this argument is acceptable, it is possible to see that the Swazi may be right when they say their great ceremony, so openly affirming conflicts, is a source of unity and strength—of cohesion. For the 'drama of kingship' states a process that is present in actual political life. It affirms the acceptance of kingship as such, as the source of law and moral order for the Swazi, against internal traitors and external foes. It does so by stating that those who are hostile to the ruling king, nevertheless support him because they support the kingship. And the possibility that the king may be personally inadequate, and may desecrate the values of the kingship, is admitted in the insults he suffers. This does not invalidate the kingship itself.

The general theme I have been putting forward emerges with great force from an account by Delegorgue, an early French traveller, of the Zulu ceremony. His account is the more telling because he did not understand what he was looking at. He described the Zulu government as despotic, and commented on the ceremony: 'It is at the time of the general assembly of warriors (towards December 8th) when the maize ripens, that lively discussion takes place. There are free interrogations which the king must immediately answer, and in a manner which will satisfy the people. I have seen at that time ordinary warriors come leaping out of their ranks, transformed into orators full of spirit, extremely excited, not only returning the fiery glance of the king, but even denouncing him before everyone, blaming his actions, stigmatizing them as base and cowardly, obliging him to explain, destroying the reasoning in his answers, dissecting them and unmasking their falsehood; then proudly threatening him and ending with a gesture of contempt.' 'I have also seen, after such discussions', Delegorgue goes on, 'I have also seen the king's party and that of the opposition on the point of hurling themselves upon one another. I have seen that the voice of the despot was no longer heeded, and that a revolution could have exploded then and there had a single ambitious man come forward to profit by the indignation of the party opposed to the king. But what surprised me no less, was the order which succeeded the end of this kind of popular tribunal.' It is the surprise of M. Delegorgue that I am trying to explain away. Clearly no revolutionary leader could come forward at that point. The attack on the king was demanded by tradition and it naturally culminated in the warriors exhorting the king to lead them to war. For the attack must have been on the king, as shown by Delegorgue's words, for failing to live up to the standards of kingship—it exhibited the conflict between the kingship and the human frailty of the king, between subjects and king. But it affirmed the value of kingship.

I could demonstrate the extent to which conflict is thus used in ritual in many other political ceremonies, both in states and in societies without governmental institutions. A remarkable example among a people without government occurs among the Tallensi of the Gold Coast. Professor Fortes has shown there that different groups are involved in a series of rites, so that each group must perform its part of a cycle of rituals if all are to be prosperous. One lot of groups is responsible for rain, another for fertility of the crops. And what is important for my purpose is that when each lot performs its rites the other must remain shut up in its homes, under pain of mystical punishment. Unity and interdependence are again stressed by mutual exclusion, to achieve prosperity for all. For this unity and this interdependence are made up by the separateness of the component groups. It is significant, too, that marriages are banned in this period, for marriages establish special links between the independent groups and conflicts within each group which I've already discussed. Herein, I venture to suggest, lies the origin of the ban on Christian marriages in Lent, and of Jewish marriages at the same period. This, in the

Mediterranean, is the period between first fruits and harvest, and the period of great national rites in the ancient civilizations. Marriages, as the source of unity across division, were taboo.

These rebellious rituals thus occur in national ceremonies and in domestic ceremonies. At the installation of a village headman in many Central African tribes he is insulted and told he is unworthy of office: the Yao strike him on the head to knock him out, ritually to kill him. Here successors to headmanship are also tested for witchcraft, because it is believed they may have killed their predecessor and their rivals. In these small political groups the struggle for power cuts deep into personal relations, and this is used in the ritual to cleanse the headman and to install him so that he may rule wisely and to the benefit of the villagers. But the statement of conflict in ritual is not carried into the smallest grouping of society, and that a very important one—the elementary family. No ceremony that I know allows the open statement of hostility by children to parents, by parents to children, or by brothers and sisters to one another. Psychologists will probably say that may be because the conflicts here cut too near the bone: the relationship could not be re-established if the conflicts repressed in these most intimate sentiments were exhibited. As a social anthropologist I seek for an explanation of a different kind. The rites I have been considering all go on in groups which endure despite the life and death of members, or their geographical movements. They are on the whole enduring groups—nations, interlinked political groups, villages, local districts of women in the Zulu goddess's ritual. The family is not such an enduring group: it breaks up with the death of the parents and with the marriages of the children. It has not the same sort of cohesion as the other groups. And the basis of my argument is that the licensed ritual of protest and of rebellion is effective so long as there is no querying of the order within which the ritual of protest is set, and the group itself will endure.

But family relationships are altered when children grow up and when they marry. Here the ritual which involves their separation from their parents does not state that the parents resent the adulthood of their children or their marriages. Commonly, the parents may abstain from being present. When a Tsonga girl reaches puberty, her mother does not attend the rites: she is looked after by a substitute mother. This in itself signifies a breaking away from her mother's apron-strings. Barotse parents do not attend their children's marriages. Absence in this way may be ritually effective in symbolizing a change of relationships; in the Tallensi political ceremonies I've quoted (where political groups which are interlinked hide when their peers are performing their ceremonies) absence is effective in allowing the ceremony to achieve the blessing of prosperity for all. Prescribed absence from a ritual is thus a form of participation in it: though it is not a protest, it states that there is a conflict present in the social process.

I myself was fortunate to observe this process vividly in certain boys' circumcision ceremonies in North-western Rhodesia. There are many similar rituals throughout South-central Africa. Earlier descriptions of these rituals all just stressed that they were taboo to women, who had to remain away.

I found that the absence of the women was part of their contribution to the ritual which aimed to help their sons grow up. By not being present they assisted their sons to break away from them, and become men, associated with their fathers. But through the ritual as a whole, the women had to abstain for periods, and then join actively in certain rites. The rites involved a symbolic marriage of men and women to give rebirth to the boys as complete men. This symbolic marriage was based on the idea that the mating of sexes for procreation involves the union of two opposed but complementary persons—man and woman. Male and female symbols were linked throughout the camp where the boys were isolated. And men and women successively fought one another, separated, united in joy at the growing-up of their sons. The ceremony was compared for me with marital relations—a 'fighting with joy', a union fraught with conflict, but a union which would be successful if the proper rites were observed, as ordained by the ancestors. Again, the open statement, the exaggeration of conflict, was believed to achieve a generally desired end—the maturity and fruitfulness of the boys. It did so because women agreed in wanting their sons to become men, like their husbands. There was no division over the ultimate rightness of the social order.

I have been arguing that the emphatic dramatizing of conflict within a particular type of social order may be believed to bless that order, so long as it is unquestioned. People are required to express their hostilities to one another so as to secure a blessing: they assert acceptance of common goals despite these hostilities. I have also suggested reasons why rituals of licence do not occur inside the elementary family. But I have still to deal with other rituals where the element of conflict is not expressed, and the aim of the ritual is secured by straightforward affirmations of unity and identity of purpose. This is a complex problem, but I believe the clue to the answer was given by Delegorgue's description of the Zulu national ceremonies. In all the ceremonies I've been describing this evening, despite the conflicts, there is no division about the desired end, and no doubt about which is the dominant moral rule or social relationship. The Zulu and Swazi states were strong and unquestioned. In domestic life, the Zulu had a very strong patriarchy, under the dominance of the eldest son of a man's chief wife. It was difficult for men to leave their paternal kin, or for women to leave their husbands. The strength of this system may allow the women's licence in ritual; as the strength of the army structure allows the Christmas reversal of rôles when officers wait on men. Similarly, in the Polish ghettoes, where the rabbis were powerful, once a year a sermon attacking them was preached in the synagogue by a wastrel; this was not found where the rabbinate was weak. In Swaziland, if the king was still a boy, the rites of rebellion were not practised. I don't know the full answer to this, but I am suggesting that where the relationships involved are weak, there cannot be licence in ritual.

The weakness of a relationship may lie in its own structure. But it may also be weak because it involves conflicts of social principles which are immediately obvious and which cannot be reconciled. Then, I think, the ritual will affirm the principles separately, and it will not stress the conflict between them.

Finally, another profitable line of inquiry seems to lie in the contrast of ritual handling of conflict with the secular handling of conflict. For example, the political conflicts which I described for the Zulu and Swazi, are also present in Barotse life. Yet the Barotse do not have rituals of rebellion. But their political system is so organized—as the systems of Zulu and Swazi are not—that all these conflicts are built into an elaborate series of councils. The conflicts are exhibited and expressed in differentiated secular relationships. And here, I believe, lies an important clue to understanding why rituals are so few in our own society. There must be many reasons for this, but I put only the lessons of rites of protest.

I have been advancing two lines of argument in my attempt to understand these rites. First, in Africa, on the whole, a man does everything with the same set of fellows—he works with them, plays with them, acts politically with them, worships with them. An intricate set of relationships is woven in which every interest for the people depends on right relationship with the same lot of their fellows. A quarrel with your brother or your wife upsets your subsistence activities, for example. Wider ties in the society are developed by extending the ties inside the family: and the result is an intricate mesh of relationships in which the same people depend on one another for many things. Custom marks out the individuality of different relationships within the whole. And the customs of ritual are used to indicate any change in the relationships, or change in the activities within them. So that the birth of a child, or a boy's attainment of maturity or marriage, a man's going hunting or the taking in of harvest, and so forth— all these change the whole pattern of social life. The intricate set of relationships is disturbed, and thus the moral order of the society. This has to be righted. And it is righted by reaffirming the general moral order, through stating both the cohesion and the conflicts which exist within that cohesion. The conflicts can be stated openly wherever the social order is unquestioned and indubitable—where there are rebels, and not revolutionaries. In such a system, the licensed statement of conflict can bless the social order.

This hypothesis of how rituals of protest can occur in certain societies, also implies why they cannot exist in other types of society, such as our own. First, we have revolutionaries as well as rebels, suffragettes as well as good wives and mothers—indeed, good wives and mothers are often suffragettes. Once there is questioning of the social order, the ritual of protest is inappropriate, since the purpose of the ritual is to unite people who do not or cannot query their social rôles. And beyond this, our society is composed of highly fragmented and divided relationships—our interests lead us into association with a whole variety of different persons, in the family, schools, pubs, work-places, churches, political organizations, recreational clubs, and so on. The dissatisfied person can change his membership of groups, vote for a new government, join a new club, seek work in a new factory, move away from his family when he marries. In African society, a man could not do this so easily; and my impression is that rites of protest are less developed in those societies where some movement is possible. Hence,

I suggest—the problem is too complex for a strong affirmation—hence, I suggest, we do not have the many rituals of Africa. They are inappropriate in the family, our single many-interest group. They are inappropriate in the state, because we have revolutionaries as well as rebels. All our other groups have voluntary and not compelled membership. And many differentiated secular institutions, with great freedom of movement, allow for the temporary solution of personal and sectional conflicts.

We don't have rituals in the sense that we believe that the acting of social rôles will in some supernatural manner affect our prosperity and unity in this way. But, of course, we have many ceremonials expressing unity. And a few of these are recognized to state conflicts. Yet I am also sometimes tempted to regard as 'ceremonies' other squabbling actions in our social life, which are usually assumed to be realistic. Parliamentary debates and election campaigns are full of dispute: I wonder how realistic much of this is, and what relation it bears to the actual taking of political decisions. Periodic scandals, say about the actions of the Civil Service, may lead to the affirmation of general principles about how the country should be run, as if there were not posed impossible reconciliations of different interests. These inquiries may not alter what actually happens, but they affirm an ideal condition of unity and justice. Even some strikes appear to be ceremonials of rebellion in the national industrial system. For some of them end, and apparently for a time happily, without changing conditions; and others lead to a change which might have been achieved without the demonstration. Yet the demonstration

K

appears to be a preliminary necessity. African society was not changing in its structure, and rituals of rebellion worked because ultimate values, some contradictory, were put on a mystical plane where they could not be questioned. Ours is a rapidly changing society. Nevertheless, I am not sure that these processes which are like those we find in Africa, may not act to persuade us that there is great persistence notwithstanding the change.

VI

THE BONDS IN THE COLOUR-BAR

IN my previous five lectures I've discussed the working of long-established societies, or of states built up by conquest over peoples of similar type. I argued that in these societies custom establishes certain conflicts between men, and may thus produce quarrels among them. Custom at least controls the places where quarrels take place. But custom also brings into work mechanisms which inhibit the development of the quarrels and which exert pressure for settlement. Or the conflicts are so directed by custom that there is change in the personnel of the system, but the structure of the system persists. Finally, I examined rituals which openly state the conflicts that exist within a social order, and yet which are believed to bless that order. I hope I have not given the impression that in old Africa all quarrels were settled amicably, and all conflicts were redressed. This is far from true. I was describing only the redressive and compensating effect of different kinds of conflicts in African societies, where the established order is taken for granted, and where there may be rebels but there are no revolutionaries.

This evening I pass to consider an entirely different kind of social system, that of modern South Africa. Here we have a nation-state which is full of quarrels firmly set in custom and belief—quarrels between

Whites and Blacks and Indians and Coloured, between
Afrikaners and English, as well as between economic
interest groups, and so forth. Does the general thesis
that conflicts in men's allegiances in one set of relationships leads to cohesion over a wider range of relations,
or through a longer period of time, apply to this sort
of society? Clearly in South Africa the system is
constantly changing, and with these changes the conflicts it contains are altering. But are the conflicts of
allegiances themselves part of such social order as
there is? I think they are.

This doesn't mean that I approve of these conflicts.
Indeed, I don't. I am one of those South Africans
who have reacted strongly against the racial dis-
crimination of our country. I claim no prophetic
vision in seeing disaster ahead of it. But I can try to
examine objectively the sort of society which South
Africa has created with the bonds of the colour-bar.
Furthermore, I am trying to understand how this
society keeps working. The divisions, the conflicts,
the hatreds, between people and groups in South
Africa are obvious enough. But how does the society
keep going: wherein resides its cohesion? The striking
problem here, as it was in feuding societies, is to show
the order, not the quarrels, to see how quarrels are
contained, not how they arise. And I find the same rule
applies which applied to feuds—divisions in the ranks
of any group, which link its members with its enemies
in other relationships, exert pressure to prevent open
fighting. But the whole system is so ill-balanced that
each settlement leads to a change in the system,
and to the breeding of new and more violent quarrels.
Though until recently there were at least some cross-

linkages between the colour-groups: later Governments have been hard at work eliminating them.

I must say again that when I find cross-linkages between the colour-groups and suggest that these produce some stability in the larger system, I am not approving or disapproving. I am only describing and analysing and seeking to explain the difficult problem: why does not South Africa explode? I have always felt that research into the causes of peace would be more profitable than research into the causes of war.

Ultimately, of course, South Africa keeps going because the Whites wield superior force. They conquered the country by force of arms, or the threat of arms, and by patently superior technology. It is true that some African tribes sought protection; but this was often against other Whites, and these tribes saw they had no choice. To some extent, this same argument applies when they sought for protection against other tribes; it was superior arms, despite the smaller numbers of the colonists, which counted. Force established the authority of the Whites, and force keeps it going—not only actual arms, but better organization, central control, greater overall unity, telephones, and so forth. I am not going to keep mentioning this point, which Hilaire Belloc summed up: 'Whatever happens we have got The Maxim gun; and they have not!' I am sure that if the Whites did not have this police and military control of organization and firepower, they would not last very long. The Africans learnt how strong are this firepower and organization, with overseas reserves, in the course of early wars and a few revolts and riots:

but it is not only the fear of this firepower which keeps them working in a whole series of relationships with other colour-groups. I say, keeps them working— may I say, *kept* them working—because I am going to talk about conditions in the mid-thirties, when I was doing social anthropological research in one part of South Africa. I then came to the conclusion that it was money, as well as guns, which keeps South Africa going. Money does so by giving Whites and Blacks reciprocal, if also competing, interests in the whole economic system; and money introduces divisions in the ranks of each colour-group. Money is the prime factor, but there are, of course, also others which are important—education, religion, political alliances, even friendship.

I feel it is more profitable to examine this problem in a small area of South Africa. I choose Zululand, in Northern Natal, primarily because I studied it, and because I do not know of another analysis which has looked at the cohesive effect of conflict in a modern African situation. I have, of course, also used other studies in making my interpretation. I have been working with the general idea that wherever men act in relation to one another, it is possible by observation to find regularities in their actions. In short, the behaviour of men in society forms a system, which has a structure. This system, as Herbert Spencer pointed out long ago, is akin to an organic, rather than to a mechanical, system. We study in society both an anatomy and a physiology. And the idea of conflicts which are resolved within the overall system of the society, and which contribute to the continued operation of that system as a whole, has physiological parallels. The whole process of eating, digestion, and excretion, exhibits the same kind of situation. But social systems, unlike organic systems, are fluid: they can change much more rapidly, and they can inter-breed. Zululand is an area where different kinds of social systems have been interbreeding, and changing after interbreeding.

Social systems can interbreed with astonishing rapidity. But they also show a great capacity for absorbing intrusions without change. Both these processes can be seen in Zululand's history. When European mariners began to pass the region on their way to India from the sixteenth century onwards, some of them were shipwrecked among the Zulu peoples. Many were killed: the system eliminated them forthwith. Shaka, the man who created the Zulu kingdom early in the nineteenth century, told British traders that his ancestors had been afraid of the Whites, whom they regarded as a particular kind of sea-monster, and killed. If his statement was true, it means that before these shipwrecked Whites were eliminated, they were first absorbed into the Zulu beliefs as monsters. But there are records of other shipwrecked sailors among some tribes who were accepted into the society as if they were tribesmen. For instance, in 1686 some Dutch sailors who had been wrecked on the Natal coast managed to get back to Cape Town. On their march they met a Portuguese who had been cast away forty years before. They reported: 'This Portuguese had been circumcised and had a wife, children, cattle, and land; he spoke only the African language, having forgotten everything, his God included'. Many Whites, men, women, and children, were absorbed thus.

One whole tribe in the Transkei is said to be descended from a White woman. Other Whites were absorbed, not as ordinary commoners, but as chiefs and councillors, in view of their apparent superior wisdom and greater technical skills. Similarly, it seems that at first the goods brought by these European ships were absorbed into the economies of the region, with only the effect of strengthening the position of chiefs. These insisted on all trade passing through their hands, but they distributed the trade-goods, as they had tribute, among their subjects. The same processes took place later on in Central Africa.

In 1818 Shaka, the head of the small Zulu tribe, conquered most of the region of Natal and established himself as king over a powerful nation of warriors. Six years later British traders settled at Port Natal, the present Durban, and began to trade with the king. They became habitués at Shaka's court, and were a source of great gratification to him. He established them as his chiefs at Port Natal: they were constitutionally absorbed into his political system. He began to use them in his dealings with his enemies, for he called on them to bring their muskets to assist his armies in fighting a tribe which was opposing his imperium. He also tried to send an embassy through them to negotiate an alliance with the British king. Here we see that the new body of British, few in numbers but powerful with firearms, and with their links to the Cape, were accepted into the system as strengthening the king in his foreign relations—they were accepted in terms of existing conflicts. Later, Shaka's brother and successor, Dingane, used the Boer trekkers who sought land from him to recover cattle which he alleged had been stolen from him by another chief. And another brother, Mpande, got the Boers to help him oust Dingane; forty-seven years later Mpande's grandson also called on the Boers for assistance in a civil war. I am citing these instances because they clearly exhibit that when the members of two societies come into relationship with one another, they quickly establish regularized relations, and the form of these relations may be shaped by internal conflicts in either society. British traders and Boer trekkers were hostile to one another; but when the Boer trekkers were massacred by the Zulu, the British turned against their patron, the Zulu king, and supported their fellow-Whites.

But once the British were established they did not continue as chiefs in the system equivalent to the king's other subordinate chiefs—though he called them 'my chiefs' at Port Natal. There began to gather about them tribesmen who had fled from the Zulu armies when these were conquering the region; and refugees from the harsh Zulu king fled to them for sanctuary. No ordinary chiefs could have granted such sanctuary. Relations between the king and his White chiefs became strained over this matter, and a missionary, Captain Alan Gardiner, R.N., had to negotiate a treaty under which the Whites agreed to accept no more refugees. In addition, these White chiefs, and the Boers, were the outliers of large White groups with a range of technology, goods, and weapons, quite superior to those of the Zulu. Their settlement completely upset the balance of power in the region. Soon there were states of a different kind established in the Zululand region, one Black and the other White.

These states were separated by a border, but many inter-relationships existed across the border. The Natal Government intervened at the request of the Swazi to stop Zulu attacks on the Swazi. Traders and missionaries and hunters went from Natal, by the Zulu king's permission, into Zululand. Their own descriptions show that they were familiar figures among the Zulu, and that standardized modes of behaviour between Whites and Zulu had evolved. These manners generally emphasized the separateness of the two colour-groups, but there were also many customs for intercommunication. I am going to skip over this period, which I've used chiefly to show how easily social systems absorb new elements into their pattern of conflict and cohesion, and how easily distinct social systems interbreed. The process of social inter-breeding emerges more clearly after the final conquest of Zululand by Britain in 1887. The Zulu state was broken, and the Zulu king became one of many chiefs ruling small separate tribes in Zululand. Native Commissioners were established with troops to support their authority.

I have read the archives dealing with this period and have discussed what happened with many old Zulu. I became deeply impressed with how quickly British rule was accepted. Zulu told me that their king Cetshwayo challenged the British envoy to one day's battle for a trial of strength, claiming that his warriors were as numerous as the hairs on a cattle-hide. Sir Theophilus Shepstone is said to have replied that British soldiers were as numerous as the grass on the hillsides. The Zulu won their day's duel, at Isandlwana in 1879; but the British brought out more troops who defeated the Zulu decisively. So the Zulu learned what very great force the British could develop despite an initial loss; and only once since the early period, in 1906, have any of them staged an armed revolt.

But many Zulu had become interested in getting peace, and they saw that only the British could establish that peace. The Zulu War had ended in 1880 with the exile of King Cetshwayo. Zululand was divided into thirteen chieftainships. Freed from the restraining order of the kingdom these chiefs began to quarrel. The British re-installed Cetshwayo over one-third of his kingdom, a cousin was left independent in another third, and a final third was placed under British protection. War broke out between the king and his cousin; the royalists attacking the cousin, and through him the British, called in Boer help. The Boers claimed in return land and cattle; the royalists turned to their previous enemies, the British, for help against the Boers whose claim was reduced. This is ordinary foreign politics. But another large slice of Zululand had been lost.

The British finally decided to assume full control. Crops had not been planted, villages had been burned, life was insecure. The *Pax Britannica* seemed a blessing to many Zulu. Yet still the new Native Commissioners had to use force to get some of their orders accepted, even among the tribes which had been their allies. Force was the final factor in establishing British rule, but while that rule put an end to certain things which the Zulu valued, it satisfied other Zulu interests, both general and particular. As the desire to get the support of British or Boer weapons in their struggles had

previously divided Black opposition to the coming of
the Whites, so this new division of interests introduced
conflicts into Zulu allegiances and thus facilitated the
wider establishment of British rule. This led to the
development of an intricate social system involving
many relationships between Whites and Blacks.

Reports of the British Native Commissioners of this
period show four main trends. First, the royalist section,
which had fought to the end and had seen the king
exiled, was described in 1891 as 'maintaining a kind
of passive resistance to my authority'. But a month
later the Commissioner joyfully reported: 'I have had
to adjudicate in two matters between prominent
members of the [royalist] party. These are about the
first cases of the kind that have been brought to me;
and the fact may be of some importance as indicating
a tendency on the part of these people towards
acknowledging and accepting the authority of the
magistrate.' With their leader in exile, possibly there
was no Zulu superior to these men to settle their
dispute, for at a meeting three years later the royalist
leaders still showed open hostility to the Government.
But the effect was as stated by the magistrate. Where
litigants refused to obey Zulu judges, only Government
could enforce its decisions, and thus settle cases among
a people used to regular judicial procedures. Government was being accepted to settle internal disputes.
Also, while at first royalist chiefs and leaders refused
stipends offered them and compensation for crops lost
in the settlement of tribal boundaries, after a few years
they accepted the money. The payment of stipends to
chiefs made it in their interest to be loyal to Government.

The second trend is that from the beginning certain chiefs were anxious to demonstrate their loyalty to Government, and deferred to the Native Commissioners. They helped to recover stolen cattle, to punish faction fighters in their tribes, to collect tax, and so forth. In 1888, just over a year after the first establishment of the magistracy, a chief who had been Prime Minister to the rebellious King, sent messengers to the Commissioner to say a murdered body had been found. They reported his words: 'When I heard of the murder I summoned the people of that neighbourhood and acted according to my old habit in Zululand in order to fathom the matter. I did not mean any disrespect to Government by investigating the matter myself. Now I have sent for you to examine the following people. . . .' This is typical of many acts by chiefs and commoners. In 1891 the Commissioner wrote to his superior that there had been reported to him many deaths from fever. He went on: 'The Natives are gradually becoming more accustomed to report their troubles to me . . .'. For the Zulu were ready enough to take advantage of Government's presence and what they could derive from it.

The third trend in these records is that the Commissioners tried constantly to make use of the chiefs in their administration. In 1889 the Commissioner asked that a chief be appointed over the royalist faction as it was 'exceedingly difficult' to administer them without a chief. Ruling through the chiefs was most economical, and money for staff was scarce. This method of rule was also quite satisfactory for Government purposes, even though the chiefs were not wholehearted servants of Government. So that, again, when in settling the boundaries of tribes Government found difficulty in making a definite allocation, it constituted a new tribe there and appointed a chief over the new tribe. A meeting of Zulu was informed: 'The present aide of the magistrate's court . . . is to be appointed. As soon as he takes over the duty his connection with the magistrate's court will cease.' It is significant for later developments, that his connection with the magistrate's court has so effectively ceased that his heir is now absorbed into the Zulu nation's resurgent opposition to the Whites. This has also happened to a tribe from British Natal which had loyally served the British during the Zulu War and was rewarded by being moved into the King's area in the heart of Zululand. This King's area had contained no ordinary villages, but only royal military barracks for the King's regiments, and it became uninhabited when the Zulu army was disbanded. But this tribe now joins all Zulu in their resentment against White rule.

The fourth and most important trend was the development of the Commissioner's work independently of the chief. He was the focus in his district of the whole Government machinery. Only he could act in matters across district boundaries, and in matters involving Whites. Especially as Zulu began to go out to mines and industries to earn money, only the Commissioner could handle many of the business and personal matters which arose for them and their kin. In tax-collecting, control of hunting, pass-laws, and like matters, a steadily increasing minimum of allegiance to the Commissioner was enforced. In 1891 chiefs lost their power to try criminal offences, and the Zulu had to rely on the Commissioner for protection against wrongdoers. But above all, the Commissioner, more than anyone else, represented White culture with its technical superiority and desirable advantages. As early as 1888 a chief asked the Commissioner to send a doctor to treat him, and in the next few years the Commissioner assisted the Zulu in several epidemics. Cattle diseases made him undertake veterinary work. He organized famine relief, built roads, shot troublesome game, handled missionaries, traders, and labour-recruiters. He began to employ Zulu in greater and greater numbers; as the chief had lost his right to collect tribute and to call up labour, he could not support his court and employed fewer and fewer men. An index of the increasing importance of the Commissioner, as contrasted with the chiefs, is that no new chieftainships have been created in Northern Zululand, while the original magisterial district has been divided into three—though obviously it was initially far bigger than any chieftainship. The Commissioners' subordinate White and Zulu staff has grown. Government brought with it a vast cultural apparatus, and it used some, though not all, European technical achievements in its administration. The first Commissioners carried out many works, and these in time came to be handled by separate technical departments —veterinary, agriculture, health, education, public works. Technical officers are supposed to consult with administrators, and do in general. But there are many conflicts between these different officers; and I wish I had time to tell the fascinating story of how Zulu try to exploit these conflicts for their own ends.

This growth in the local organization of Government went with many cumulative changes in the life of the

Zulu. Peace was established. Zulu wanted money to pay taxes and buy the coveted goods of the Whites: most of them had to go out to work. They began to adopt White tools. Schools were opened and missionaries began to win converts to Christianity, as they had not been able to do under the Zulu kings. An Anglican missionary of the earlier period is reputed to have said: 'The only way to get Zulu Christians is to buy 'em and breed 'em'. The dependence of Zulu on an economic and political system established by the Whites increased steadily. Thus there emerged in Zululand a social system containing Blacks and Whites which had a cohesion of its own, arising from the common participation of Zulu and Whites in economic and other activities in which they became more and more dependent on one another. Force established White rule and the threat of force maintained it. But the Zulu want of money, and their desires for White goods and education, created a system of social relationships in which Whites and Zulu co-operated to earn their separate livings. Even White force was used to protect individual Zulu against breaches of law by other Zulu, and by Whites. The system contained many sources of dispute and friction, but these arose largely out of new forms of co-operation between the colour-groups.

It was the drive of the expanding White group which established this joint system of relationships, and which determined its form. Under it, the Zulu became largely peasants and wage-labourers, periodically entering distant industry to earn money and leaving the tribal areas where their families worked the land. But Zulu traditional territorial groups were absorbed into the system as administrative units, and chiefs as subordinate officials. Blacks and Whites, despite their co-operation, were sharply separated by custom and language, standards of living, types of work, marriage barriers, and social exclusiveness. But they were held together largely in the cohesion of a common social system— by money and cultural ties, as much as by the Maxim gun.

For my main argument, I want to emphasize that the system worked because from the beginning divisions of interest in the Zulu group led certain of its sections and individuals to seek alliances with certain White groups or individuals. Zulu kings sought the aid of White muskets against their Black enemies. Later, desires for peace, for White technical assistance, and for White money and goods, introduced conflicts in Zulu allegiances, and thus led some Zulu—eventually almost all Zulu—into co-operation with Whites. The whole process of establishing cross-linkages across the main Black-White division was quickly at work. Rarely did Zulu and Whites face each other only as solid, united groups in hostile relations—not even during the Zulu War when two sections went over to the British. The individual Zulu who sought co-operation with Whites did so partly out of conflicts in the Zulu group: they were chiefs who were hostile to the king; subjects who resented the rule of chiefs; younger sons who were not going to inherit the family herd; women who fought against patriarchal control of their marriages; ambitious commoners who saw more scope in service for the Commissioner than for the chief, and in education rather than in peasant cultivation. Similar divisions in the White group were

L

operating. Missionaries who wanted to evangelize, educate, and improve Zulu approached them with interests very different from Boer farmers: churches of Zulu and Whites worshipping together arose. Traders and recruiters had other interests. Through these years the bonds of co-operation crossing the colour-bar were bonds between different sections in each group, for each group's members were divided by conflicting interests and values. And these conflicts existed in individuals who pursued various, and often conflicting, ends, in the new social system. These conflicts within each group and each individual led to cohesion in the emerging larger system.

This is an outline of the historical developments which produced the Zululand I studied in the middle thirties. In *that* Zululand, the Zulu accepted their Native Commissioners because they represented the White Government with its overwhelming backing of force and the technical superiority of the White group. The Government, with missionaries' help, had established peace, encouraged men to go out to work for Whites, supported schools, started health, veterinary, and agricultural services, and had brought in through traders many goods ardently desired by the Zulu. The Native Commissioner was the centre of the complicated machinery which directed the working of these new enterprises. He therefore not only applied Government regulations, mostly unwelcome, but he was also the chief local head of the organization which was helping the Zulu to make some adaptation to new conditions—not all unwelcome to all Zulu. He was able to do much that the chief, still leader of his people, couldn't do for lack of power, organization, and knowledge. People went to the Commissioner constantly with queries and troubles. Thus he had come to stand for many of the new values and interests which were influencing Zulu.

But while individual Zulu, and groups of Zulu, acknowledged and used the Commissioner, their attitude to Government was mainly suspicious and hostile. They blamed it for the new conflicts which had emerged in their own community. They pointed to restrictive laws. They regarded even measures which Government appeared to intend in their interests as being designed to take from them their land and their cattle; and they cited in argument the encroaching of Whites on Zululand in the past, and what they regarded as a series of broken promises about their land. They did not trust any proposal emanating from Government—or any White man. My Zulu servant said to me: 'White men treat Blacks as they treat fish. The first day they throw meat into the water, and the fish eat it: it is good. The next day there is a hook in it.' And I have seen an old Zulu, after some of them had been discussing the very effective cattle-sales introduced by the then Commissioner, hold his hands apart—'a White project is like this, and then' (reversing his hands around) 'we learn what is behind it. We Zulu will sell all our cattle, and then we shall cease to be a people.' A Zulu agricultural demonstrator complained to me that life was unpleasant for him as the people treated him as a spy (*ifokisi*—a fox). I heard a chief upbraid this demonstrator for coming to ruin his district, but the same chief pointed out to me how much better the maize in the demonstrator's garden grew than the maize in his own garden. He explained to me: 'I am not such a fool that I cannot see his methods are better than mine; but if we followed his methods the Whites would see that our land is good and take it away from us, as they have done before. We must not let them see how good our land is.' For this reason, or rationalization, chiefs opposed the damming of a valley which would have brought prosperity to a dry region.

Thus the initial reaction of the Zulu in any situation in which Government officials proposed beneficial schemes, was to reject them. The result was that their chiefs, whom they expected to lead their opposition to Government but who were required by Government to assist it, were caught in insoluble conflicts. This position was clearly exhibited in 1938 when a chief who opposed the building of cattle-paddocks with rotational grazing was praised by his people, but condemned by Government officials. On the other hand, a chief who asked for cattle-paddocks was praised by officials, but condemned by his people. For the people look to their native leaders to examine Government proposals and 'stand up for the people' against them.

The Zulu are ready enough to express these feelings of opposition. They have a legend (I could not discover whether it is based on fact)—that when General Hertzog succeeded Smuts as Prime Minister and Minister of Native Affairs he came to Zululand to address a meeting. When he had finished speaking, no Zulu rose to reply. Finally, on the invitation of the local Commissioner, their own Prime Minister spoke. He is reported to have said: 'This

chief has spoken pretty words. We have listened, but
we do not know what they have to do with us. We do
not know this White man. Who is he? We were
defeated by the English and became subjects of Queen
Victoria. The English handed us over to the Boers,
without consulting us. We are not children to be
handed about thus, and do not recognize the change.'
Again, in 1938, the Paramount Chief, then recognized
by Government as social head of the Zulu nation,
called a great meeting of Zulu to hear the report of
their elected members of the newly formed Native
Representative Council. He began by telling the
crowd, which included many Whites, that he was a
nominee of the Government on this Council: therefore
they had not come to listen to him, for he was 'a spy
of Government' (an *ifokisi*). A great shout of laughter
relieved the Zulu's apprehension that he was in fact
a Government man.

Thus I found that Commissioner and chief had
opposed positions in the modern political structure of
Zululand. The chief's powers had been radically
curtailed; he had lost his relatively enormous wealth;
he was surpassed in the new knowledge and skills by
many of his people; the men had less time to devote to
his interests; he could no longer levy tribute or labour.
He could enforce only that allegiance which Government, in its desire to rule through chiefs, would make
his people render. True, his disapproval was a serious
sanction; but it could be faced. If he tried to oppress
or exploit a man, this man could turn to the Commissioner for protection. But the chief had found a new
basis for his power: to lead his people in their resistance
to Government and to the Whites. If he too readily

accepted Government proposals which he might well believe to be in his people's interests, they would turn against him.

But the chief not only led his subjects' opposition to Government. He also joined with them in a way no White official could do. The Commissioner could not cross the barrier between Black and White. He could talk with Zulu and discuss their troubles, but his social life was with the other Europeans in his district. And, of course, he had no kinship or marriage ties with Zulu. On the other hand, the chief's social life was with his people. He was related to many of his subjects by kinship ties and any of them might become so related by marriage. Though the chief was their superior, he was equal with them as against the Whites and (in their own words) 'felt together with them'. They told me: 'The chief has the same skin as we have. When our hearts feel pain, his heart feels pain. What we find good, he finds good.' No White man could do this, could represent them. For chiefs appreciated with other Zulu the value of many customs which were decried by Whites.

Beyond this, the Zulu were ignorant of world history and it had no emotional value for them: the chiefs, and especially the Paramount Chief descended from their great kings, symbolized their traditions and values.

The first great defeat by the Boers of the Zulu under King Dingane at Blood River in 1838 on December 16th, is now a South African national holiday—Dingaan's Day. For the Whites it celebrates a great victory, which for the Zulu was a great defeat. But for the Zulu their kings stand for victories over other tribes, and over British and Boers, which they remember with pride equal to that of Whites in their traditions. When I knew the Zulu, they acknowledged their chiefs' position partly through conservatism and partly because Government recognized the chiefs. But a chief was also usually chief by tradition and inheritance. Zulu said: 'The chief has the blood and the prestige of chieftainship and they extend to his relatives: the Commissioner has only the prestige of his office, and his relatives are nobodies'. By this contrast the Zulu expressed the chief's position as it existed independently of Government's acknowledgement, and rooted in their values and traditions.

In carrying out this research I obviously could not commonly discuss these problems with the Zulu: it would have been impolitic. Anyway, I was only another White man, with some well-concealed profitable motive behind my interest in them and my friendship with them. (They would feel they were right if they knew of my present position.) But I gradually built up this view of the opposition of Commissioner and chief by watching the behaviour of Zulu and Whites in many diverse situations, and listening to their conversations. Indeed, my first conclusion was that opposition and hostility were absolute. But as I sat in chiefs' courts or at tribal meetings, and at the Commissioner's headquarters, I also became increasingly aware of the large amount of co-operation and cohesion. Chief and Commissioner were opposed, but in routine administration they worked together fairly well. Chiefs and their subordinate officers actively assisted the Commissioner in the administration of law and the carrying out of certain executive duties. The Commissioners were keen on their work and anxious to see their districts progress; indeed, some of them came into opposition against other Whites, and even against the Government that they represented, as they pressed measures in the interests of Zulu. And as individuals some of them won the trust of their people. But it was never complete, and the attitude of suspicion to Government as a whole and to Commissioners as authorities remained unchanged.

This attitude rarely came into the open, and then only over major issues. In day-to-day life the system worked. When major issues arose the superior power of Government could force a measure through unless it depended on the willing co-operation of chiefs and people. The Zulu, then, had little hope of resisting Government rule and passively accepted decisions, even if they avoided implementing them. At meetings of tribal councils they expressed their hostility. The proud, unquenched resentment of the Zulu under their subjugation has been magnificently embodied in Roy Campbell's poem, *The Zulu Girl*, where he speaks of

> The curbed ferocity of beaten tribes,
> The sullen dignity of their defeat.

I became aware thus of the routine functioning of the system. In time I observed something beyond this. The opposed balance between the authorities of Commissioner and chief shifted from situation to situation in Zulu life. A certain minimum of allegiance to both Commissioner and chief was enforced by Government; the influence of each might vary above that minimum with their characters and relations to each other. A sympathetic Commissioner who understood the Zulu would draw them to him, especially from an unsatisfactory chief; a harsh Commissioner kept the people away from him, and they went more to their chiefs. Even more I observed that the balance shifted for different individuals in the same situation, or for the same individual in different situations. A man who considered the chief biased against him, favoured Commissioners as impartial; but for him the chief was the source of justice when the Commissioner enforced an unwelcome law. The people rallied to the chiefs to oppose measures such as cattle-paddocking. If the chief tried to impress their labour, they compared him unfavourably with the Commissioner who paid for the labour he employed. They would say, however, at other times, that the Commissioner gaoled people for slight offences to get free convict-labour and that was the purpose of prisons—then later they would praise imprisonment as the most sensible way of handling wrongdoers. The Zulu were constantly comparing Black and White political officers and switching their allegiance according to what was to their own advantage, or by what values they were being guided on different occasions. This switching of allegiance was not a matter of attitude only, but of action: I've largely deduced the attitudes from the actions.

Thus I found in the political system of Blacks and Whites some of the same processes that existed within the Zulu group. For the equivocal position of the Zulu chief in the relations between Government and people was an extreme form of the equivocality that attends

M

every position of authority in an administrative system of this type. The officer represents the superior power to those below him: he represents those below him to the superior power. The situation was sharpened for the modern Zulu chief (or Baganda king) because there were such great differences in the values and interests of White and Black groups. The chief stood in this system in the same position as the village headman within a Zulu tribe: as the man at the bottom of the Government's hierarchy, moving among those ruled, he took the brunt of the conflict between authority and subjects. But the chief was drawn by his own skills and traditions for maintaining order and giving justice into co-operation with the Commissioner. He had special interests, in his stipend for example, in giving this co-operation. And he was pushed by the interests of some of his people in the new system into giving that co-operation, even though in other situations they expected him to oppose co-operation. A series of many conflicts developed the shape of modern Zululand polity, so that that polity worked—it had cohesion arising out of the conflicts.

In their actions towards these political leaders the Zulu did not form an undifferentiated group. The greatest division was into pagans and Christians. Christians, or schooled people, were in general readier to accept White innovations than pagans were; thus the Zulu group was divided into two groups, which were sometimes hostile to one another, though in most situations the individuals concerned co-operated as kinsmen and neighbours. Indeed, pagans often accepted innovations from a Christian relative which they resisted from Whites themselves. Missionaries entered into this situation as friendly though suspect characters: they remained on the other side of the colour-line. The majority of Christians had the same attitudes and acted as the pagans, operating similarly according to the situation. But their complaints against Whites and Government were often different from those of pagans. They tended to object, not to innovations, but to the slow pace of innovation. Some of the best educated among them, having come most strongly against the colour-bar, reacted away from White culture and reverted to their old culture, which they attempted to revive. There were also other sub-groupings, such as magistracy clerks, Zulu police, and Zulu technical assistants, who had special ties with Government. And overall there was the interest of all Zulu, as individuals and as breadwinners for their families, in earning some money for food, clothes, and the other means of subsistence, which led them to work for Whites. Thus they came into dependence on Whites. In this process Zulu met Whites in factories, churches, and White houses—for colour-groups did not meet as whole opposed blocks, but in smaller groupings and relationships within which their interests divided their allegiances from the standard loyalty of Zulu as against Whites. Conflicts of allegiance in the Zulu group were operating to produce cohesion in the larger system. Similar divisions and conflicts of allegiance were operating in the White group. The Commissioner was prepared to face Parliamentary hostility in Cape Town in order to do his job well in Zululand.

The central cleavage into colour-groups influenced almost every relationship. Missionaries evangelized Zulu who entered into churches with them: in response there developed separatist Zulu Christian sects reacting against White control. Simple paganism was not enough to oppose the churches, though some separatist churches embody pagan beliefs in their doctrines. Political associations split similarly. New conflicts in the Zulu group drove some people to accept White innovations, and involved some development of Zulu beliefs. The cult of the ancestors became obsolescent as family-heads tried to keep their Christian as well as their pagan kin. Beliefs in witchcraft and magic, which, unlike the ancestral cult, were not tied to relationship between kin, were applied in the many new relationships with strangers. At all points conflicts were influencing the large-scale, fragmented, but working, social system which was emerging. In the towns and the rural areas, groups embracing tribes to whom the Zulu were traditionally hostile emerged, and the Zulu chiefs had to establish linkages with trade union leaders, national congress leaders, and so forth. But all these groups were divided both by old loyalties and by new divisions of interest, leading to constant co-operation with Whites, so that continual open quarrelling was prevented.

I have been describing how conflicts within the Zulu and White groups broke into the solid loyalty of each group, by linking together sections and individuals. These conflicts divided the Zulu in their opposition to Whites, and introduced infirmity of purpose in each individual Zulu. But the conflicts were not by any means well balanced; and when a particular difference with a White had led to a change of action on the part of the Zulu he did not find that he had solved his immediate problem. He was faced with the same problem still, or with a new problem. There was neither an accepted social system in which Zulu and Whites could come to satisfactory terms nor a moral order they would both accept. The colour-bar still divided them.

Therefore the ability of the Zulu to play off Commissioner against chief in different situations did not enable the Zulu to solve the problems of poverty, deteriorating land, inadequate wages, cultural strain, restrictive controls, and so forth, which they considered oppressed them. Ultimately neither set of authorities could meet their needs. Changes of the incumbents of offices, alterations of jobs, movements to new areas—no shifting of allegiances—could redress the fundamental cleavage of the colour-bar. Each new situation led not to the re-establishment of the old system, but to a changed system. The deep conflict which split the black-white society of Zululand within the Union of South Africa has continued to develop with aggravated severity.

My own observations in Zululand have been confirmed by those of many anthropologists, and other impartial observers, in several parts of Southern Africa. Government Commissions have validated these conclusions. Similar situations are found in East and West Africa, though developments have varied with many factors—the number of settlers, whether they entered as a citizen army or after a professional body of troops, whether they are artisans or farmers or industrialists and how strong each of these groups is, what was the organization of the indigenous African societies, how the new African élite was treated, and so forth.

I am interested in the African situation as a son of Africa. But I have this evening been using the situation of Zululand to illustrate my central argument—that conflicts in one set of relationships lead to the establishment of cohesion in a wider set of relationships. I thought it best to do so with one detailed analysis. I have left aside many variations. And I have not even touched on the towns where Africans are employed and increasingly settle, though it is largely in the towns that the direction of present developments is determined. Zululand is an illustration, not a complete miniature, of modern Africa.

What I have tried to show is that the old Roman maxim, 'divide and rule', is not necessarily the Machiavellian trickery of self-seeking conquerors or rulers. Sociologically, the principle might be stated as, 'divide and cohere'. Hence I've called this analysis 'the bonds in the colour-bar' not because the Africans and Indians of South Africa are chained by discriminatory custom; but because discriminatory custom against the Africans and other coloured groups chains the dominant White group. This dominant group is separated so sharply from the other colour-groups that it loses its ability to manoeuvre and to establish links of friendship with Africans who, in other situations, may well be opponents. In the past, segregation policies were not applied consistently, and in social life consistence of logic counters systematic cohesion. I myself saw—and enjoyed—many friendly relationships between Whites and Blacks during the first years of my life, and while I was doing research in the field. But as the policy of *apartheid* is applied more and more consistently, any sort of amicable or loyal relations between Whites and Blacks become impossible. Those sections within the White group which were linked in some friendly relationship with sections of the Black group, are being attacked. This is symbolic of deepening, irresoluble, unbalanced conflict. If these sorts of links are eliminated, Black will deal with White only as authoritarian ruler and employer, always as an enemy, and never as an ally.

READING LIST

GENERAL:

1. Allan, W. *Studies in African Land Usage in Northern Rhodesia*, Cape Town: Oxford University Press, Rhodes-Livingstone Paper 15 (1949). (A theoretical analysis of African agriculture, with two specific studies.)
2. Colson, E., and Gluckman, M. (editors). *Seven Tribes of British Central Africa*, London: Oxford University Press for the Rhodes-Livingstone Institute (1951). (General accounts of seven tribes studied by modern anthropologists.)
3. Schapera, I. (editor). *The Bantu-speaking Tribes of South Africa*, London: Routledge (1937). (Eighteen chapters on various aspects of the African peoples.)

LECTURE I. THE PEACE IN THE FEUD

The lecture was based mainly on:

4. Evans-Pritchard, E. E. *The Nuer: A Description of the Modes of Livelihood and Political Institutions of a Nilotic People*, Oxford: Clarendon Press (1940); and *Kinship and Marriage among the Nuer*, Oxford: Clarendon Press (1951). Also his *The Sanusi of Cyrenaica*, Oxford: Clarendon Press (1949).
5. Colson, E. (i) Essay on Mazabuka Tonga in *Seven Tribes of British Central Africa* (item 2); (ii) 'Rain Shrines of the Plateau Tonga of Northern Rhodesia', in *Africa*, xviii (1948); and (iii) 'Social Control in Plateau Tonga Society', in *Africa*, xxiii (1953).

166

6. Fortes, M. *The Dynamics of Clanship among the Tallensi*, London: Oxford University Press for the International African Institute (1945).

7. Fortes, M., and Evans-Pritchard, E. E. (editors). *African Political Systems*, London: Oxford University Press (1940). (See 'Preface' by A. R. Radcliffe-Brown, Editors' 'Introduction', and essays on Bantu Kavirondo, Tallensi, and Nuer.)

8. Nadel, S. F. *The Nuba*, London: Oxford University Press (1948).

LECTURE II. THE FRAILTY IN AUTHORITY

The lecture was based on:

9. Barnes, J. A., Mitchell, J. C., and Gluckman, M. 'The Village Headman in British Central Africa', in *Africa*, xix (1949).

10. Evans-Pritchard, E. E. (i) *The Divine Kingship of the Shilluk of the Nilotic Sudan* (Frazer Lecture, 1948), Cambridge University Press (1948); *The Political System of the Anuak of the Anglo-Egyptian Sudan*, London: Percy Lund, Humphries, for the London School of Economics and Political Science (1940).

11. Fortes, M., and Evans-Pritchard, E. E. 'Introduction' to *African Political Systems* (item 7).

12. Gluckman, M. (i) 'The Kingdom of the Zulu of South Africa' in *African Political Systems* (item 7, and essays on Ngwato, Bemba, Ankole, and Kede by various authors in this volume); (ii) essay on 'The Lozi of Barotseland in North-western Rhodesia' in *Seven Tribes of British Central Africa* (item 2); (iii) *The Judicial Process among the Barotse of Northern Rhodesia*, Manchester University Press (1955).

*Devons, E. *Planning in Practice*, Cambridge University Press (1950).

See also:

13. Cunnison, I. *History on the Luapula*, Cape Town: Oxford University Press, Rhodes-Livingstone Paper 21 (1951).

14. Herskovits, M. *Dahomey*, New York: Augustin (1938).

15. Kuper, H. *An African Aristocracy: Rank among the Swazi of the Protectorate*, London: Oxford University Press for the International African Institute (1947).

16. Nadel, S. F. *A Black Byzantium: The Kingdom of the Nupe of Nigeria*, London: Oxford University Press for the International African Institute (1942).

17. Schapera, I. (i) *A Handbook of Tswana Law and Custom*, London: Oxford University Press (2nd Edition, 1955); (ii) *Tribal Legislation among the Tswana*, London: Percy Lund, Humphries, for the London School of Economics and Political Science (1943); and (iii) *The Political Annals of a Tswana Tribe*, University of Cape Town, School of African Studies: Communications, new series, No. 18 (1947).

17a. Wilson, G. *The Constitution of Ngonde*, Livingstone: Rhodes-Livingstone Institute, Rhodes-Livingstone Paper 3 (1939).

LECTURE III. ESTRANGEMENT IN THE FAMILY

The lecture is based on:

18. Evans-Pritchard, E. E. (i) *Kinship and Marriage among the Nuer* (item 4); and (ii) *Some Aspects of Marriage and the Family among the Nuer*, Livingstone: Rhodes-Livingstone Institute, Rhodes-Livingstone Paper No. 11 (1945).

19. Fortes, M. *The Web of Kinship among the Tallensi*, London: Oxford University Press for the International African Institute (1949).

20. Gluckman, M. 'Kinship and Marriage among the Lozi of Northern Rhodesia and the Zulu of Natal' in *African Systems of Kinship and Marriage* (item 21, succeeding).

21. Radcliffe-Brown, A. R., and Forde, C. D. *African Systems of Kinship and Marriage*, London: Oxford University Press for International African Institute (1950). (See especially 'Introduction' by Radcliffe-Brown, but also all nine essays on various tribes.)

22. Richards, A. I. (i) *Land, Labour and Diet in Northern Rhodesia*, London: Oxford University Press for International African Institute (1939); and (ii) *Bemba Marriage and Modern Economic Conditions*, Livingstone: Rhodes-Livingstone Institute, Rhodes-Livingstone Paper No. 4 (1940).

23. Schapera, I. *Married Life in an African Tribe*, London: Faber & Faber (1940).

See also:

24. Barnes, J. A. *Marriage in a Changing Society: A Study in Structural Change among the Fort Jameson Ngoni*, Cape Town: Oxford University Press, Rhodes-Livingstone Paper No. 20 (1951).

25. Forde, C. D. *Marriage and the Family among the Yakö*, London: Percy Lund, Humphries, for the London School of Economics and Political Science (1941).

26. Gulliver, P. H. *The Family Herds*, London: Routledge & Kegan Paul (1955).

27. Holleman, J. H. *Shona Customary Law*, Cape Town: Oxford University Press for the Rhodes-Livingstone Institute (1952).

28. Kaberry, P. M. *Women of the Grasslands* (Bamenda, British Cameroons), London: Her Majesty's Stationery Office, Colonial Research Publication No. 14 (1953).

29. Mayer, P. *Gusii Bridewealth and Customs*, Cape Town: Oxford University Press, Rhodes-Livingstone Paper No. 18 (1950).
30. Peristiany, J. G. *The Social Institutions of the Kipsigis*, London: Routledge (1939).
31. Phillips, A., Mair, L., and Harries, L. *Survey of African Marriage and Family Life*, London: Oxford University Press for the International African Institute (1953).
32. Wilson, M. *Good Company: A Study of Nyakyusa Age-Villages*, London: Oxford University Press for the International African Institute (1951).

LECTURE IV. THE LOGIC IN WITCHCRAFT

The lecture is based on:

33. Evans-Pritchard, E. E. *Witchcraft, Oracles and Magic among the Azande of the Anglo-Egyptian Sudan*, Oxford: Clarendon Press (1937).
34. Mitchell, J. C. (i) *The Yao Village*, Manchester University Press for the Rhodes-Livingstone Institute (1956); and (ii) 'The African Conception of Causality' in *Nyasaland Journal*, iv (1951).

See also:

35. Krige, E. J. and J. D. *The Realm of a Rain-Queen: A Study of the Pattern of Lovedu Society*, London: Oxford University Press (1943).
36. Marwick, M. G. 'The Social Context of Cewa Witch Beliefs' in *Africa*, xxii (1952).
37. Mayer, P. *Witchcraft*, Inaugural Lecture to the Rhodes University, Grahamstown, South Africa.
38. Nadel, S. F. (i) Chapter VI in *Nupe Religion* (item 47 below); and (ii) 'Witchcraft in Four African Societies: An Essay in Comparison' in *American Anthropologist*, 54 (1952).
39. Wilson, M. *Good Company* (item 32).

LECTURE V. THE LICENCE IN RITUAL

The lecture is based on:

40. Fortes, M. *Dynamics of Clanship among the Tallensi* (item 6).

41. Gluckman, M. (i) *Rituals of Rebellion in South-East Africa* (Frazer Lecture, 1952), Manchester University Press (1954); (ii) 'Zulu Women in Hoe Culture Ritual' in *Bantu Studies*, ix (1935); and (iii) 'The Rôle of the Sexes in Wiko Circumcision Ceremonies' in *Social Structure: Essays Presented to A. R. Radcliffe-Brown* (ed. M. Fortes), Oxford: Clarendon Press (1950).

42. Junod, H. A. *The Life of a South African Tribe* (Tsonga), London: Macmillan (1927), Volume II.

43. Kuper, H. *An African Aristocracy* (item 14).

See also:

44. Colson, E. (i) 'Clans and the Joking Relationship among the Plateau Tonga of Northern Rhodesia' in *Kroeber Anthropological Society Papers*, Nos. 8–9, Berkeley, California, (1953); and (ii) 'Ancestral Spirits and Social Structure among the Plateau Tonga' in *International Archives of Ethnography*, xlvii (1954).

45. Evans-Pritchard, E. E. *Nuer Religion*, Oxford: Clarendon Press (in press).

46. Forde, C. D. (editor). *African Worlds: [Nine] Studies in the Cosmological Ideas and Social Values of African Peoples*, London: Oxford University Press for the International African Institute (1954).

47. Nadel, S. F. *Nupe Religion*, London: Routledge & Kegan Paul (1954).

48. Sundkler, B. G. M. *Bantu Prophets in South Africa*, London: Lutterworth (1948).

LECTURE VI. THE BONDS IN THE COLOUR-BAR

The lecture is based on:

49. Bryant, A. T. (i) *Olden Times in Zululand and Natal*, London: Longmans (1929); and (ii) *The Zulu People*, Pietermaritzburg: Shuter & Shooter (1949).

50. Gluckman, M. (i) 'The Kingdom of the Zulu of South Africa' in *African Political Systems* (item 7); (ii) 'Analysis of a Social Situation in Modern Zululand' in *Bantu Studies*, xiv (1940); (iii) 'Some Processes of Social Change Illustrated with Zululand Data' in *African Studies*, i (1942); and (iv) *An Analysis of the Sociological Theories of Bronislaw Malinowski*, Cape Town: Oxford University Press, Rhodes-Livingstone Paper No. 16 (1949).

51. Ritter, E. A. *Shaka Zulu: The Rise of the Zulu Empire*, London: Longmans (1955).

See also:

52. Allan, W., and others. *Land Holding and Land Usage among the Plateau Tonga of Mazabuka District*, Cape Town: Oxford University Press, Rhodes-Livingstone Paper No. 14 (1948).

53. Barnes, J. A. *Politics in a Changing Society: A Political History of the Fort Jameson Ngoni*, London: Oxford University Press for the Rhodes-Livingstone Institute (1954).

54. Busia, K. A. *The Position of the Chief in the Modern Political System of Ashanti*, London: Oxford University Press for the International African Institute (1951).

55. Epstein, A. L. (i) *The Administration of Justice and the Urban African*, London: Her Majesty's Stationery Office (1953); and (ii) *Juridical Techniques and the Judicial Process*, Manchester: University Press, Rhodes-Livingstone Paper No. 23 (1954).

56. Hellmann, E. *Rooiyard: A Sociological Study of an Urban Native Slumyard*, Cape Town: Oxford University Press, Rhodes-Livingstone Paper No. 13 (1948).

57. Hellmann, E. (editor). *Handbook on Race Relations in South Africa*, Cape Town: Oxford University Press for the South African Institute of Race Relations (1949).

58. Hunter, M. *Reaction to Conquest: Effects of Contact with Europeans on the Pondo of South Africa*, London: Oxford University Press for the International African Institute (1936).

59. Kuper, H. *The Uniform of Colour: The Influence of Western Civilization on the Swazi of the Protectorate*, Johannesburg: Witwatersrand University Press (1947).

60. Mair, L. *An African People in the Twentieth Century* (Baganda), London: Routledge (1934).

61. Mitchell, J. C. *African Urbanization in Ndola and Luanshya*, Lusaka: Rhodes-Livingstone Institute, Communication No. 6 (1954).

62. Richards, A. I. (editor). *Economic Development and Tribal Change: A Study of Immigrant Labour in Buganda*, Cambridge: Heffer, for the East African Institute of Social Research (no date: 1954).

63. Schapera, I. (i) *Native Land Tenure in the Bechuanaland Protectorate*, Alice (South Africa): Lovedale Press (1943); and (ii) *Migrant Labour and Tribal Life: A Study of Conditions in the Bechuanaland Protectorate*, London: Oxford University Press (1947).

64. Wilson, G. *An Essay on the Economics of Detribalization in Northern Rhodesia*, Livingstone: Rhodes-Livingstone Institute, Rhodes-Livingstone Papers Nos. 5 and 6.

65. Wilson, G. and M. *The Analysis of Social Change*, Cambridge University Press (1945).